S0-AQL-143

THE POWER
OF THE
PLATFORM

SPEAKERS ON LIFE

www.LVCSB.com
Las Vegas Convention Speakers Bureau

THE POWER OF THE PLATFORM
Speakers on Life

Published by TwoBirds Publishing, Inc.
and
Las Vegas Convention Speakers Bureau
www.LVCSB.com

2657 Windmill Pkwy, #116, Henderson, NV 89074

Copyright © 2010 TwoBirds Publishing, Inc.
Library of Congress Control Number: 2010921783
ISBN-13: 978-0-9754581-7-4

All rights reserved. No part of this publication may be reproduced, stored in a retrieval system, or transmitted in any form or by any means without the written permission of the publisher.

Cover Design and Formatting by
Julia Lauer, Ambush Graphics
Editing and Composition by
Robin Jay & Michelle Johnson

Special Note: This edition of "The Power of the Platform - Speakers on Life" is designed to provide information and motivation to our readers. It is sold with the understanding, that the publisher is not engaged to render any type of psychological, legal, or any other kind of professional advice. The content of each article is the sole expression and opinion of its author, and not necessarily that of the publisher. No warranties or guarantees are expressed or implied by the publisher's choice to include any of the content in this volume. Neither the publisher nor the individual author(s) shall be liable for any physical, psychological, emotional, financial, or commercial damages, including but not limited to special, incidental, consequential or other damages. Our view and rights are the same: You are responsible for your own choices, actions, and results.

Printed in the United States of America

10 9 8 7 6 5 4 3 2 1

ACKNOWLEDGEMENTS

I'd like to thank the **coauthors** for their trust. You've enabled me to share incredible messages of inspiration, motivation, and business how-to with readers around the world.

Publishing an anthology is a tremendously collaborative effort. I can't imagine doing it without the help, advice, and support of the incredible "Diva" – Michelle Johnson. Michelle owns **Diva Las Vegas Productions,** an event production company. I am blessed that she takes the time to help as my grammatical editor. She makes me laugh – even when we are both seriously sleep deprived.

Julia Lauer, owner of **Ambush Graphics**, is an incredible artist and typesetter. Her eye for details is extraordinary. Finding someone who is a pleasure to work with is even rarer.

Special thanks to Brian Tracy. In the midst of his current adversity, his thoughts are on how others may benefit from his experience; that's the true heart of motivational speaker. Brian, I wish you the very best.

~ Robin Jay

FOREWORD

Choosing to live each day with passion comes easily for many people. For others, life's road is rocky. I have lived both. Having an anthology like *"The Power of the Platform"* gives us a chance to share our lives and benefit from each other's experiences. I jumped at the opportunity to contribute the foreword to this book. I hope that no one ever has to deal with the challenges that I have had in my life; it's my desire to share the knowledge I've gained by coming this far.

My best friend Harissa was killed in a car accident in 1989. I buried my anguish – although my grief manifested itself as an eating disorder and depression. In August 2000, my best friend Troy died in a cliff diving accident. I was affected deeply. I became angry at life and at God for taking this wonderful man. When I spoke to his parents, we all prayed together. Somehow, through it all, I found my relationship with God – which later proved to be essential to my survival.

Then, on June 12th, 1994, my sister – Nicole Brown Simpson - was murdered. My pain was indescribable and overwhelming. For the next ten years, I worked in corporate America. In September of 2004, I was engaged to be married when - just four days before the ceremony – my fiancé cancelled our wedding.

That loss triggered an emotional tailspin. I became self-destructive and so clinically depressed that I could not get out of bed. I was paralyzed – spiritually and mentally.

I was magnificently angry. I drank too much and self-medicated. I was a ticking time bomb of confusion, grief, devastation, and negative emotions. Finally, at a family gathering a few weeks later, I exploded. Every emotion I'd ever suppressed in my entire life came spilling out violently. I lashed out at my loved ones, devastating some of the most important people in my life.

Later, alone in my bedroom, I held pills in my trembling hand. I wanted the pain to end. Yet, somewhere deep inside me, I realized that I didn't want to die. I could sense that I was here for a greater good. It was at that moment that my sister Dominique entered my room. I told her, "Get me away from here." The next morning, she helped me to take my first step toward healing: acknowledging my inability to cope and wanting to get help.

I was admitted to the Behavioral Health Department in Laguna Beach, California, where I was an inpatient for 10 days and then an outpatient for two months. From that one-time experience, I learned how much mental illness affects everyone in a family. My mother asked, "Do I have to watch another child die?" I told her I knew this treatment could save my life. I was fortunate; many of us never discover the tools we need to embrace life for the miraculous gift that it is.

I was taught journaling, time management, goal setting, stress reduction, breathing techniques, meditation, and other tools to help me manage and then control my life. I learned techniques for eliminating co-dependency, self-doubt, self-sabotage, and limited thinking. I would journal my thoughts and feelings every day. I purged all the emotions that had been locked inside me for so long.

I learned the importance of laughing and how to feel gratitude for the beauty that surrounds us. Armed with valuable tools, experience, and knowledge, I now help inspire others to CHOOSE LIFE.

Today, as a certified mental health and wellness coach and public speaker, I help individuals, businesses, and communities focus on developing positive mental health and wellness. I support the important goals of the **With Hope Foundation**, which works to help prevent teen suicide.

My deepest passion is to educate, inspire, and motivate people so that no one has to remain in a space of anger and despair. I want everyone to be free to live the life of their dreams.

~Tanya Brown

For more information on Tanya and her services, contact her at:

www.tanyabrown.net
Tanya@tanyabrown.net

TABLE OF CONTENTS

INTRODUCTION

Mentors for the Heart, Mind, and Soul

In December 2009, I came across Robin Jay's video on *"The Art of the Business Lunch."* I liked what she had to say about the business lunch, so I posted it on my blog. Robin found it, thanks to Google Alerts – notices that are automatically sent to you whenever your name comes up anywhere on the internet. She visited my blog and posted a comment, thanking me for sharing her video with my visitors. **That e-mail changed my life – literally.** We started corresponding and she sent me copies of the first two e-book editions of *"The Power of the Platform."*

Robin offered me support and encouragement and told me how much she enjoyed my writing. It was exciting to hear an expert say that I had talent. We tend to question ourselves, so it was **very satisfying for me to have that validation.** I have worked very hard pursuing my passion.

Building an Author's Platform

I began writing my novels for ***"The Munroe Series"*** in August of 2008. A few months later, I started blogging on Wordpress and joined several writers' forums. I discovered that if I was going to be a writer and author, I would also have to develop an *"author's platform."* I did not have the foggiest idea what that meant, so I did some research.

In the course of my research, I was surprised to find that many "best selling authors" had outdated blogs that were not labeled properly for Google. The Internet operates in a very different language than any other medium. Search engines such as Google and Yahoo recognize certain key words and promote them; they know what information is current and relevant and archive whatever is outdated.

I decided I would help them out. I created a blog to promote other writers, authors, and best-selling books. On my site, ***TheIdeaGirlSays. wordpress.com,*** I promote interesting people, projects, book trailers, motivational speakers, and fan-made videos.

Establishing My Reputation

My goal was to establish myself and become a published author. I set out to connect with other writers, book cover artists, editors, literary agents, and publishers and learn something from all of them.

I also wanted to tap into the entertainment world because I love music, movies, celebrity news and artwork, so I created another Wordpress blog and called it "Idea Girl Consulting."

The more visitors you have on the Internet, the more visitors you will get. I post videos on my **Idea Girl Consulting YouTube Channe**l, and I insert my blog URLS into each of the videos. Along with this, I promote my articles on Blog Catalog, Facebook, Twitter, Bing, Google, and other sites.

In June 2009, I achieved Squidoo.com's status of **"Giant Squid"** for having more than 50 websites on Squidoo. Over the next few months, I continued to win writing awards, including the "NaNoWriMo – National Novel Writing Month" challenge for my novel *"The Calamity Girl – The Promotion,"* and the "Script Frenzy" challenge for my screenplay *"Forgive Me; I'm Not Perfect."* In spite of my blogging success, I was beginning to doubt whether I'd ever get published! That's when I met Robin, and I found a new source of encouragement.

Discovering Personal Development and Feeling its Power

Robin and I began to correspond regularly. I continued to blog about *"The Art of the Business Lunch."* In February, 2010, she sent me paperback copies of her lunch book as well as the first two *"The Power of the Platform"* books - *"Speakers on Success"* and *"Speakers on Purpose."*

Reading these books has changed my life drastically! I relished the diverse information and motivation that the various speakers had to share.

Jack Canfield wrote how success begins with believing in yourself. *After reading his chapter, I began to have more faith in my projects and myself.* **Dr. Nick Hall** wrote about facing your fears – whether they be fear of success OR fear of failure! **Charli Douglass** wrote about the Universal Laws of Success, including the Law of Attraction. **Andy Ebon** wrote about blogging your way to business success by creating an online "face" and personality. He explained how you could expose the *soul* of your company. **Jim Fannin** focused on self-discipline.

As you can see, the information in the chapters was as varied as it could be. There were chapters on **change, attitude, business, sales,** and **living your best life**. I found the messages from the coauthors to be informative and inspiring.

The Difference Having a Mentor Can Make

Robin Jay was so inspiring to me in her emails. When I finally found the courage to tell Robin that I was not just a blogger but also a writer, she read my work and told me that I was an awesome writer, and that I was extremely creative. ***Can you imagine what that meant to me at the time?*** Are you telling the people in YOUR life what they are doing right? It is so important that we have this type of support and encouragement.

Valuable Writing Tips from an Unexpected Mentor

There were times when I was down or discouraged, and Robin would encourage me to stick to it. I sent her my manuscript for **"*The Calamity Girl - The Promotion*"** to get some feedback, even though I was terrified at the thought of what she might say. In my mind, her opinion would determine whether I would keep writing or not. I was that close to giving up on my dreams.

Thanks to Robin, **I did not give up.** She gave me some very valuable advice about writing and it changed my life. Most importantly, she continually took the time to read my work and offer her thoughtful criticism.

She looked at the first chapter of my manuscript and wrote, *"You are very creative and colourful; I think you could write professionally – but the "stream of consciousness" writing that works in a blog needs a bit more attention when writing fiction or non-fiction."*

This line intrigued me! It was the first time I realized how different writing a blog is from writing a novel. Now I understood why my manuscript did not have the proper tone or rhythm to it. The information she shared completely changed how I write.

Robin showed me the importance of consistency when using tenses in my writing. She said it was not as crucial an issue when blogging, but that I needed to pay more attention to it when writing my books. "Were you **looking** at something? Or did you **look** at something?" Changing tenses back and forth in the same sentence can be confusing to a reader. Finish your thoughts!" she wrote.

Robin recommended that I put myself in the mind of my readers to make sure that everything is CLEAR. She told me that readers should not have new information hitting them unexpectedly, and that I should not assume that they know what I am thinking. She encouraged me to check and double check to make sure that I fully (but not tediously) explain myself.

The Light Bulb Went Off!

Finally, someone had revealed what my problem was. I had not been able to figure out what was wrong with my manuscript. I had been jumping from one scene to another without warning, leading the reader to get lost in a new set of circumstances.

I often blog about movies and complain when a plot or story line is choppy and people or events just "appear." I began to see the similarities between writing and motion picture editing. Robin said lastly, "Be as SPECIFIC as possible in describing your situations, emotions, actions, etc." I loved this advice; it gave me the freedom to get even more creative.

Suddenly, everything became clear for me. I tackled my manuscript with zeal and fixed it chapter by chapter. Now that I have a clear, concise story line, editors will find my novel easier to deal with and will be more willing to publish my work.

Beyond the gift of Robin's excellent advice, **I have also received great lessons from the coauthors that are in the anthologies.** *The speakers in these books have become my personal mentors.*

It is important that we look for a diamond in the rough. Robin saw something in my work that told her I was on the right path. I am forever grateful for her words of wisdom and her kindness of heart. I hope that you, too, will take the time to encourage and support the people in your life who need to know that they are doing good work and are on the right path as well.

###

Linda Randall is a writer, blogger, and author. Blogging about today's top celebrities, movies, music, artists, writers, and motivational speakers has put Linda on top of most search engines. She also creates book trailers and features new musicians on her blogs.

For more information, visit Linda at her blogs:

Twitter:
@theideagirl

Blogs:
theideagirlsays.wordpress.com
ideagirlconsulting.wordpress.com
www.helium.com/users/281492/show_articles
www.squidoo.com/lensmasters/lindarandall

As the beloved originator of the **Chicken Soup for the Soul®** series, **Jack Canfield** watched the series grow to a billion dollar market. This alone makes him uniquely qualified to talk about success. Jack is also the author of the best-selling *The Success Principles: How to Get from Where You Are to Where You Want to Be.*

Affectionately known as "America's #1 Success Coach," Jack is America's leading expert in creating peak performance for entrepreneurs, leaders, managers, sales professionals, employees and educators. Over the past 30 years he's helped hundreds of thousands of individuals achieve their dreams.

Jack is a Harvard graduate with a Master's Degree in psychological education and is one of the earliest champions of peak performance. He has a gift for sharing his methodology and results-oriented activities to help others produce breakthrough results. For more information on booking Jack for your next event, please visit:

> *Website: www.JackCanfield.com*
> *E-mail: teresa@jackcanfield.com*
> *Facebook: JackCanfieldFan*
> *Twitter: @J_Canfield*
> *Phone: 805-563-2935*

Chapter One

How to Turn *Limp Affirmations* Into Mantras for Success!

Jack Canfield

To *affirm* something is simply to declare that it is true. So, creating and using affirmations should be a breeze, right?

Actually, the true art of the affirmation is both subtle and profound. Despite the popularity of this technique, some people use affirmations that are bland and perhaps even self-defeating.

When creating your affirmation, remember that even minor variations in wording can make a huge difference in the results you get. Since your words literally have the power to create your circumstances, invest a few minutes now to take your affirmation skills to a higher level.

Consider the following statement:

I will quit smoking with ease and joy, remembering the effects on my physical and mental health while preparing to live a longer life.

By using the guidelines found below, you can transform limp affirmations like that into mantras for manifesting a huge change in your life!

15

The following points are key:

Five Guidelines to Follow

1) Enter the "now"

Start your affirmation by entering the present tense. Take the condition you desire and declare it to be already true.

2) Be positive

Our sample affirmation keeps the focus on smoking - the condition that you do *not* want. Instead, shine a light on what you *do* want - to be smoke-free.

A related reminder: Our subconscious mind skips the word *not*. So, delete this word from your affirmations. "I am not afraid of public speaking" gives us the message that you are afraid. Use, "I feel at ease as I speak in public."

3) Be concise

Shorter is better. Affirmations with fewer words are often easier to recall, especially in situations where you feel some stress. Rhyming makes your affirmations even more memorable. For example, "I am feeling alive at 185."

4) Include action

Whenever possible, affirm yourself as a person who takes action. For example: "I am gratefully driving my new Porsche along an open highway."

Action engages the Law of Attraction, creating new results in our lives and opening us to further inspiration.

5) Include a feeling word

Powerful affirmations include content and emotion. Content describes the specific *outcome* that you desire. Emotion gets to the heart of how you *feel* about that outcome. For a more potent affirmation, add both elements.

Consider this affirmation:

"I am supporting my children to fully come forward into the world."

The content of this statement is clear. Yet it lacks an emotional charge.

Breathe life into this affirmation by adding an active expression of feeling:

"I am lovingly supporting my children and encouraging them to fully express their unique talents and gifts."

You will know that you have a powerful affirmation when you feel a surge of emotional energy. The force of feeling jumpstarts you into action.

An Affirmation Makeover

Now get some direct experience with "affirmation transformation." Return to the first example mentioned in this article:

"I will quit smoking with ease and joy, remembering the effects on my physical and mental health while preparing to live a longer life."

Playing with the guidelines listed serves up some more exciting options, such as:

"I am breathing effortlessly with lungs that are pure and clean."

"I am celebrating how easily I breathe through strong, healthy lungs."

Also consider the following affirmations on a variety of topics:

"I am joyfully celebrating my graduation from college with a master's degree."

"I am effectively delivering my first talk to an audience of more than 1,000 people who affirm my message with a standing ovation."

"I am confidently checking the balance of my bank account as I make a deposit of $1,000,000."

"I am walking up on stage to receive my first Emmy award and receiving a roar of applause."

When you're satisfied with the wording of your affirmation, start using it right away.

Remember to Repeat your Affirmation at Least Three Times Daily

Repeat your affirmations at least three times daily—first thing in the morning, midday, and just before you go to sleep.

Regular repetition will gently return your focus to manifesting the life of your dreams.

Raquel Moscarelli's background features more than fifteen years in sales, training, management, and business ownership. Her practical experiences transferred fluidly to her work as an intuitive healer specializing in hospice care. Her ability to connect with individuals through clairsentience and clairaudience has provoked powerful experiences in individuals and groups alike.

Raquel has gained a global perspective by traveling to more than thirty countries and based on these experiences has made it her personal quest to assure that all beings have access to healthy drinking water, and has committed to donate 7% of the proceeds of her signature book "Birthmark" to the Omega Center for Sustainable Living (OCSL) www. eomega.org.

Website: *www.livingyourbirthmark.com*
E-mail: *raquel.moscarelli@me.com*
Facebook: *raquelmoscarelli*
Phone: *978-239-6682*

Chapter Two

Sidelined

Raquel Moscarelli

As children we delight in displaying our talents. I remember this from my childhood and I get to see it every day with my twin sons. They are quite opposite in terms of where their attention turns when they are left alone in "free play." My husband and I try to support their interests that are not only different from each other, but different from the way we were raised.

Today, many parents and educators embrace these kinds of clues to how an individual child should be encouraged. Unfortunately, we seldom do the same for ourselves as adults. The things that we loved – that came to us so naturally in our youth – we now downplay or discard entirely. As our innocence progressed to experience, many of us lost touch with our soul's true purpose – what I call our "birthmark."

Our birthmark is our internal sense of knowing. It might have been shut down by those who were threatened by our freedom or come as our personal reaction to not knowing how to handle unpredictable events. But we were born with free will. We can discover and live our birthmark by breaking the cycles of "dis-ease" to which we have been exposed. Science is discovering that we are more susceptible to illness when we are not in line with our destiny, so once we are able to liberate our trapped energy we will be free to live in a world of unlimited potential.

I have lost two of my dearest family members to tragic circumstances. My brother, a **Sports Illustrated-ranked #1 quarterback**, took his own life, and my mother succumbed to the confusing labyrinth of paranoid schizophrenia.

I relate my own personal experience to share with you what I now know: No matter what your history consists of, you can re-orient your life and you can make new choices. You can live according to your core principles, as opposed to those ideas you may have *received in childhood* or that may have originated from an outdated version of yourself.

What You Were Meant To Do

How many times have you seen stories of self-discovery? From the venture capitalist who found life-enriching satisfaction as the leader of an online community to the web designer whose true passion came from helping people create meaningful wedding ceremonies to the lawyer whose pro-bono work landed him his dream job as a photojournalist, the list of people who have triumphed over what I call their "received identities" – or the life we were "told" to live – goes on and on. Sometimes we may gently come to the realization that we are not living our "birthmark." But all too often, something more abrupt occurs. It is at that point that our courage and our questioning can set us on the path to freedom.

To further this process, I have trademarked a five-step program called "Living Your Birthmark™." It begins with recognizing that a "received identity" is actually an injury to our true self – our Birthmark. This injury places a person on the **sidelines**. While sidelined, they wait and watch others live their lives.

What we as individuals decide about our future while on these sidelines is crucial however, because a fateful crossroads awaits us. At that point, we either choose to follow an **exit strategy** or we decide to "live our birthmark" via a path marked by **miracles of all sizes**. If we choose the latter, we become "survivors" worthy of the word. Our lives may not look like what we thought they would, but they can feel right and be right.

Let's look at each of these stages individually:

Injury

We all know people who have received serious injuries in life, but why are some individuals able to embrace crisis as an opportunity while others succumb to self-pity? This question lies at the heart of "Living Your Birthmark™." These injuries are not necessarily physical disabilities; more frequently the "injury" is to one's received identity or self-esteem. When my father asked my mother for a divorce, for example, it started her terrifying slide into confusion about who she was. Your injury could be a business failure or a falling out with an old friend. It might be our bodies aging, where our reliance on our youth and beauty is no longer possible.

Whatever alters our self-concept, with nothing to immediately replace it, can provide a glimpse into our formerly obscured birthmark. The key to this phase of the process, however, is realizing that nothing that is right for us moving forward can ever be lost.

Sidelines

Injured players retreat to the sidelines and watch other people play the game. They may, like true team players, try to help those who are still on the field see what they are missing. But more often, when we are injured, we criticize and act out of despair. We believe that we could be doing better if we were the ones out there. We believe that the fact that we aren't is due to our own bad luck or someone else receiving favoritism.

When we are on the sidelines we have a choice: we can sulk and engage in self-defeating thoughts such as "I could never do that, so why even try?" and subsequently miss life's opportunities, (which present themselves every day - see "Miracles of All Sizes" below) or we can tap into the intuition that our life is not on its right course and realize that we could be living a purer version of ourselves.

The second choice is a wonderful beginning. Embracing this knowledge, rather than choosing to escape via an exit strategy, is the next step in the process.

Exit Strategy

You know you are using an exit strategy if a particular activity, individual, or thought reduces your interest in the rest of the world around you instead of opening you up to it. Shopping, eating, drinking, sleeping, too much or too little of anything can give you enough of a high to get you through periods of discomfort.

But the problem with "addicting out" of the pain is that you don't learn anything. When a painful cycle recurs you are simply tempted again to retreat into behaviors or beliefs that pacify or soothe you – as opposed to going into that place of feeling, which is where the real message lies. By paying close attention in the darker moments of our lives, we can glimpse flashes of genuine inspiration...we can encounter miracles of all sizes and achieve a healing that can conclusively put our losses behind us.

We all love to waste time with our "guilty pleasures," but an exit strategy is much more serious than a bad made-for-TV movie; it's **when your life turns into a bad made-for-TV movie!** No one is expected to operate at their peak performance all the time. But we all know the difference between having dessert a few times a week and downing a tub of double chocolate chunk ice cream every day, letting our gym membership lapse, and putting our "thin clothes" away in the attic. This is all part of an exit strategy; it's that moment when we stop trying.

Miracles of All Sizes

How does one find their Birthmark? The process can be subtle or it can be dramatic; it can come from a loved one's bout with illness or it can be triggered by a scene in a movie. You will find yourself resolving to be a little more alive to the mystery unfolding all around you.

On my journey I have been witness to many "coincidences" – or synchronicities; something caught my eye or I had a conversation with a stranger who inspired me. I have read a moving passage in a book or heard something unique, and I have felt that I am exactly where I should be, doing exactly what I should be doing. In this phase of "Living Your Birthmark™," we catalogue miracles of all sizes that continually touch our lives when we are ready to receive them. These miracles help us to find the strength to show up *authentically* in the world, ready to engage in our true purpose.

Living Your Birthmark™

There is no perfect path to discovering your injury, making the best use of your time on the sidelines, resisting your exit strategies with humor and resolve, or embracing miracles of all sizes. In most cases, a conscious approach simply begins with asking yourself questions about your interests and your sense of fulfillment or purpose. One common feature to the "Living Your Birthmark™" process is that those who complete it and discover their true Birthmark know they have arrived because they are ready to give back.

I hope you are inspired to take the next step! I look forward to connecting with you regardless of what stage you might consider yourself to be in. There is no reason for you to stay sidelined. Your Birthmark is waiting for you to claim it. I'm here to help you with inspirational stories of individuals who are truly living their birthmark!

 Rachel Magario is a "Brazilian Blind Visionary," who has championed over adversity consistently throughout her life. In fact, her nickname is "Rachel 9 Lives." She came to the United States to pursue her studies.

Rachel's ability to motivate audiences with her "Can Do!" attitude on all topics goes beyond borders; she is fluent in English, Spanish, and Portugese. She charms the world with her multi-cultural background.

Rachel pursued her MBA and a Masters in Interaction Design to fulfill her desire to make the world a more accessible place. Her topics include Marketing, Design, Attitude, and Human Relations. She is a kidney transplant survivor, an entrepreneur, and one of the most driven people you'll ever meet.

Website:	*www.RachelMagario.com*
E-mail:	*Rachel@RachelMagario.com*
Twitter:	*@RachelMagario*
LinkedIn:	*RachelMagario*
Phone:	*785-691-8875*

Chapter Three

Crossing the Bridge of Fear

Rachel Magario

You probably wouldn't think of being blind as having an advantage. It can, however, help to avoid distractions. Without sight, it is easier for me to ignore the apparent dangers around me.

Sometimes, we all must turn a blind eye or a deaf ear to the road blocks that lie between us and our intended destination. We can't let fear get a grip on us or keep us from achieving our goals.

If you've ever felt that you have too many problems and are so overwhelmed that you think you aren't going to make it through another day, don't give in. I have felt that way more than once and I am still here. If I can make it, you can, too!

Coming to the United States

When I was nineteen years old, I moved to the United States from Chile, chasing my dreams. I received a scholarship to study at The University of Kansas. As a blind and international student, I faced many trials. I had to improve my knowledge of basic English in order to study, I had to identify with the new culture, and I had to understand and assimilate new ways of doing things.

I had to adapt to a talking computer and assistive technology that I never had before. But it was all fun. I relaxed with sports, kept up a good social life, and I studied hard so I could do well in my classes. Life was good.

The world as we knew it

In 1998, the weekend before finals, I was coming home from an interview I had done with a journalism student who was writing about life as a blind person. My seeing-eye dog, Hamlet and I entered the crosswalk on the campus and a speeding car struck us.

The results were catastrophic; Hamlet had internal bleeding and I suffered two cracked vertebrae, a concussion, and lost all but 30% of my kidney function. Recovery was hard. I cleaned up my diet, tried various treatments, and eventually thought I'd be okay.

A few years later, my kidneys got the better of me. September 11th, 2001 was a tragedy for all Americans, marking their lives in different ways. It was also a horrible day for me.

As the World Trade Center towers were crashing down in New York, both of my kidneys failed. While most of the world was scrambling in panic, I, too, felt that my life may be over soon. Unable to stand, I crawled into my house from the backyard where I had gone earlier, hoping to feel the sun shine on my skin for possibly the last time.

When my sister stopped by to check up on me and tell me about the attacks on the Towers, she found me lying down in a terrible state. Later, in the Intensive Care Unit, I remembered an experience from years before.

See no evil, hear no evil

I was with a group of psychotherapy students, doing an exercise designed to help us appreciate what it takes to confront, manage, and overcome fear. As psychotherapy facilitators, this was a useful tool we could later use to help others manage and understand their fear.

We were expected to cross a dangerous train trestle. Not everyone was able to make it across the bridge. Many of the members had to crawl to get across. I boldly made my way without giving a thought to the danger. That was the first time I crossed it. Then, something interesting happened.

Those of us who had successfully negotiated our way to the far side rested before heading back. During that break, I heard the members talk about their experiences crossing the bridge, sharing how terrifying it was. The canyon floor was more than five stories below us and the trestle was narrow.

Even though I had known it was dangerous, the risk and the fear were not real to me. It was not until I heard others describe *their* fear in great detail, **backed by emotion**, that the reality of the danger became apparent. I let their fear permeate my sense of well being and I became afraid.

Heading back across the bridge, I became aware of how high we were above the canyon floor. I felt the wind against my face and the coolness of the sun setting. I had made it halfway back across the bridge before I froze.

I could hear a woman approaching with a steady pace. The click-clack of her heels against the railroad ties caught my attention. I asked my instructor for details. He explained that this woman was apparently on her way home, carrying groceries, and that she was walking across the bridge as though she was strolling down a street. She was simply doing what she had to do to get where she wanted to go. I took a deep breath and said, "I'm ready," and proceeded across the bridge.

I overcame my fear, inspired by this woman going about her business. I felt that if she could do it, I could do it. I focused on her instead of my frightened classmates.

Years later, as I lay in the ICU remembering how I crossed "The Bridge of Fear," I knew I had to just shut my ears to all of the possibilities for negative outcomes. I just had to face the challenge.

Days at the Beach

People ask me if I ever think, "Why me?" I probably have asked that at some point, but because of the way my life has unfolded, I have learned many things that the average person may never come to know. The blindness is just one of the many lenses through which I look at life. It is not who I am. I learned that early from my brother Renato.

When I had sight, I would follow Renato to the ocean and we'd swim. I would run after him in the soccer field. I would play with my sister Rebecca on my bike or roller skates. We would all dance, run and jump wildly.

After I became blind, Renato would take me to the beach. There, he would let go of my hand and run backwards watching me, singing out loud and telling me to follow him. I would put my hands out in front of me, afraid, and he would say, "Come on! You are just blind...you still have legs - GOOD ones – so be grateful and use them to run! There is nothing here; just sand and the ocean. Come! Come!"

Renato would shout, "If I tell you to jump, you have to jump." I thought he was testing me, even when there was nothing in front of me, just to see my response time. But one time I decided not to respond and I ended up hitting my toe on a coconut shell. My toe hurt, but my brother laughed saying, "I told you to jump! Does it hurt?" He checked my toe and then kept running, calling for me to follow him.

It was really fun. I felt free again and I learned to trust, thanks to my brother's "tough love." He helped to prepare me to cross my Bridge of Fear.

When times are tough and fear strikes, there is no time to ponder, "Why me?" The train will eventually come, and it might be too late to move. Therefore, accept that you are in the middle of the bridge and take action - one step at it time. Before you know it, you will have made it through.

The Bridge of Pain

We each cross a "Bridge of Pain" at challenging points in our lives. The good news is that once **_we make the decision to cross the bridge_**, we become free to move forward and get on with our lives.

Love yourself enough to go through the challenges that life hands you. There is much you can give to others, no matter what your circumstances may be. Don't try to be like anyone else or behave as someone else dictates you should behave. We are all unique and we are all needed.

I learned this lesson in dealing with my illness. I will always be a transplant patient and blind. I broke my vertebrae, but I can still walk. I hit my head, but I can still think. I have to take medications for the rest of my life, but **so what? I am still alive!** I give my best each day, crossing the bridges that lay before me.

Looking Forward

Years have passed since I crossed the scariest bridge of my life. If you would have told me back in 2001 that I would one day discover a passion for marketing and strategy, let alone that I would have a Masters in interaction design, an MBA, a brand new kidney, a handsome husband, a charming new seeing-eye dog named Nettie, and that Hamlet would be happily retired after nine years of faithful service, I would have laughed at you.

Life showed me that I was wrong to think that any of that was impossible. Experiencing the dichotomies of the visual and non-visual world first-hand gives me an advantage when it comes to designing mainstream technology that is accessible to everyone, and it is rewarding for me to share my stories with audiences. You too can make it across the bridges that lay before you. I am sure of it.

Doug Smith, a former 2nd pick overall into the NHL, is the author of *"Thriving in Transition."* After a broken neck and spinal cord injury ended Doug's professional career, he transformed himself through books and early internet adoption, building a new career as a successful entrepreneur and business leader in technology and manufacturing.

Ron Wiens has devoted his career to helping leaders effect real, sustainable, bottom-line enhancing change. He is the founding partner of Totem Hill, a firm focused on helping organizations build high-performance cultures. Ron's latest book is *"The Leaders Guide to Corporate Culture as Competitive Advantage"*.

Doug and Ron work as a team, taking executives through a process of personal transformation, enabling them to build a work culture that will elevate their organizations to the top of their game. Contact Doug and Ron at:

Doug Smith Website: www.dougsmithconnected.com
Doug Smith E-mail: doug@dougsmithconnected.com

Ron Wiens Website: www.totemhill.com
Ron Wiens E-mail: ronwiens@totemhill.com
Phone: 613-294-3766

Chapter Four

Phenomenal Outcomes
For the Individual and the Organization

Doug Smith & Ron Wiens

Doug shares: Like the blade of a skate cutting a line through the cold, hard ice, change is sharp. It does not happen over time; change occurs in an instant.

Blinded by the sheer impact, my body collapsed on itself with my head resting on my gloves. I didn't know it yet, but the head-on collision with the boards had just shattered my 5th and 6th cervical vertebrae in more than 100 places and had torn all of the ligaments in the back of my neck. I should have been dead, like a bird hitting a window in full flight, but I was conscious and aware. My life changed in an instant, and I began the search for a phenomenal outcome.

This was not the first time I had experienced a painful transition, only to be told by experts that a phenomenal outcome was not possible; it wouldn't be the last time either. The challenge with any of us achieving a better-than-average outcome is that we tend to use our "will" and our ego, rather than hand things over to our imagination and belief. It's natural for us to want to accept responsibility and feel in control. But at our core, we don't believe we can pull it off and our limited beliefs deliver poor outcomes.

Realizing our greatest potential requires that we embrace our imagination and let ourselves believe in the infinite power that is available to all of us. By tapping into that power, we can reach our full potential and realize phenomenal outcomes. We have already been given everything necessary to **create the picture** of what we desire and to **achieve it**. It comes into focus as we think about it, move towards it, remain open to other perspectives, and never, ever quit.

The Ego

After 25 years of being conditioned to play a specific role, everything about how I defined myself as a person had suddenly been taken away. In a flash, the *ego which had carried me through a thousand battles had become an anchor which would slowly drag me to the bottom if I allowed it to*. The honeymoon with my professional hockey career was over. How could I hold on to, harness, and focus the powerful emotions I possessed and use them to help override the illusions and physical barriers that I was faced with during this latest transition?

Support for the Phenomenal Outcome

"Support exists only if you believe it exists. If you do not believe it exists, it will never be found or accepted." —Doug Smith

The fact that I was able to play professional hockey at all was my first experience with phenomenal outcomes. At the age of two, doctors discovered that I had soft-tissue deformities that twisted my legs, and that my left kneecap was in two pieces. My mother made the difficult decision to put me in full leg braces. This was the first time I felt the contrast of confinement and the difficulty of being seen as physically disabled. At that stage of my life, you would not have been able to find any doctor or individual who believed I would ever become one of the top athletes in the world within the next fifteen years. No one that is except my mother ... and I believed her. Fortunately, many people who saw me struggling to stand up would tell this child in leg braces that he could do it, and I believed them, too.

Years later, when I was paralyzed from the chest down, my wife Patti told me that I would get up and walk again – with our newborn child – and I believed her. She was right. I have found that belief, in its simplest form, is incredibly powerful. Believing others when they encourage and support you can convince you that they are right! "What if it really IS that easy?"

If you agree that everyone benefits from this form of support, then I ask you, "Who are you supporting today, who did you support yesterday, and who will you be supporting tomorrow?" We can optimize transitions for every person, every team, every business, and every organization to varying degrees. We each have the opportunity to harness this power which we cannot see; this power of belief, trust, and support.

The Communication Factor

As the cost of speed and space on the internet drops to zero and the World Wide Web transitions to an extension of the human mind, our ability to creatively use this extension will now require ongoing personal and organizational transition. Learning to deal with transition is now directly related to the level of performance you achieve, and the prosperity your organization will experience. So how do you build an organization that is able to tap into the competitive advantage of ongoing transition that will take your organization to the top of its game? You start by building belief.

The Quick and the Dying

Ron weighs in: In the Old West, they used to say, "There are just two types of people – the *quick* and the *dead*." Today, the phrase might be, "There are just two types of organizations – the *quick* and the *dying*." Our "knowledge economy" has introduced a new set of rules when it comes to managing and leading. The *Quick* recognize this and embrace a culture built on belief as the path to high-performance. The *Dying* are hanging on for dear life to the ways that have brought them success in the past.

The Internet has taken us into a digital world where people are connected not only to each other but also to each other's knowledge. In 1975, the cumulative, codified knowledge of the world doubled *every seven years.* The prediction is that before the end of the current decade, this knowledge will double **every ELEVEN hours!** *The shelf life of* **knowledge** *will be the same as that for a* **banana.**

Competitive advantage today lies in an organization's ability to exploit this explosion of knowledge. Knowledge is a resource locked in the human mind. People can not be forced to create or share knowledge. Every individual possesses unique insights that can only be put to use with his/her active cooperation. Getting that cooperation is key to success in the modern economy. This means that the critical driver of economic prosperity is having leaders who can build an organizational culture that engages and leverages their "knowledge workers." *The modern leader's job is to build an environment that gets the knowledge workers working together, freely giving up their knowledge in order to move their organization towards its desired future.* There are three steps that leaders must take to build such an environment.

The Three Intelligences of Success

Emotional Intelligence: *Ability to connect with one's strengths and weaknesses > Belief in Self > Courage for Change*

The first step is to **help people to believe in themselves.** Today's winning organizations have employees who are invested in taking their organization to new places. This dynamic occurs naturally when employees believe in themselves and have the courage and confidence to try new things. They learn from their mistakes and move on. When they get stuck, they are the first to recognize it and they freely ask for help. Their ability to ask for help makes things go faster. The degree to which people believe in themselves is a measure of your organization's **Emotional Intelligence** (EI).

Relationship Intelligence: Ability to connect with others >Belief in Others > Trust

The second step is to build an organization in which people *care about each other*. How can caring affect an organization's performance? James Autry, former CEO of the Publisher Group, eloquently said "I need to know that you care before I care to know what you know." **Caring is the basis of trust.** If I know that you care about me and my success, then I can trust you. If I can trust you, I can speak openly and frankly with you. If I can speak openly and frankly with you, we can solve problems together. If we can solve problems together, then we can leverage each other's creativity and knowledge, and in so doing, accelerate our organization forward. The ability of your people to have a trusting belief in each other is a measure of your organization's **Relationship Intelligence** (RI).

Cultural Intelligence: Ability to develop a shared vision > Belief in the Organization > Meaning of Work

The third step that leaders must take is to *instil common cause*. When people are deeply connected to cause, they deliver extraordinary results. There is genuine caring about the success of the whole. This caring is the source of power that drives the organization and the individuals within it to incredible heights.

Cause defines an organizations culture and keeps it focused by providing incentive to change. Without common cause, an organization is like a ball in a pinball game – bouncing around hoping to score well. Without cause, this year ends up looking a lot like last year. Cause needs to be made explicit – constantly discussed and thought about. In winning organizations, employees believe in their organization and what it is trying to achieve. The strength of your people's belief in your desired future is a measure of your organization's **Cultural Intelligence** (CI).

In the knowledge economy, organizations need leaders that are capable of building a community of people who are plugged-in, turned-on, and in-tune with their organization. You do this by building your organization with people who believe in themselves, believe in each other, and believe in what the organization is trying to achieve. This represents a transformation in how we lead.

Patricia M. Annino, Esquire, is the author of the highly acclaimed book, ***Cracking the $$ Code: What Successful Men Know And You Don't (Yet)***.

Patricia is in demand nationally as a speaker for womens' organizations on topics that empower and educate women.

Patricia was voted by her peers as **One of the Best Lawyers in America**. Her talent and expertise in the practice areas of corporate and media law make her an invaluable resource. She is often quoted by news sources including the Wall Street Journal, Chicago Tribune, Morningstar, Bloomberg Personal Finance, Investors.com, and Marketwatch.

Patricia's other books include ***Women & Money: A Practical Guide to Estate Planning*** (recommended reading by the Wall Street Journal) and ***Women in Family Business: What Keeps You Up At Night?***

For more information, please visit:

Website: www.patriciaannino.com
E-mail: patricia@patriciaannino.com

Chapter Five

A Key Secret To Success:
Know Your Worth and Get it in Writing

Patricia Annino

Model Lauren Hutton revolutionized the way models get paid. Previously, models were paid an hourly wage. But in 1975, when Revlon wanted to hire Hutton, she changed the game.

Hutton had read a *New York Times* article about baseball pitcher Catfish Hunter in which he said he was going to pursue a million dollar contract because baseball was a youth-oriented business, where career spans were short.

"I was either 31 or about to turn 31," Lauren said, in a May, 2009 **Vogue** interview. "Veruschka had retired; Twiggy had retired; Jean Shrimpton had retired. All the stars were gone. Fashion photographer Dick Avedon had no choice but to work with me continually. I yelled over to my boyfriend and asked 'How do you get a contract?'

"He didn't even take a second to yell back: 'Don't do any makeup ads. Just refuse to do it. Tell all your photographers you want a contract.'" Dick Avedon understood that Hutton wouldn't do cosmetic ads without a contract. It took just six months for her plan to work.

"For six months, I worked all day," Hutton explains, "I was always triple booked. Just no cosmetic ads." Hutton stated that it took six months to work out what would be the first modeling contract ever, and that all subsequent modeling contracts were based on that.

When you enter into a contract with another party, you are taking that business relationship to a more formal level. It can be a very effective exercise, especially for women, because it forces you to write down in black and white ***what you think you are worth*** and how you are going to get paid.

If you have your own business and are sending out contracts to customers, those terms set the value. Women especially tend to undervalue themselves. Sending written contracts out minimizes that risk, as the financial terms are already in the hands of the potential customer and it is then a lot harder to undercut the price they themselves have set.

Do the research

When negotiating a contract, the first step is to figure out what you are worth to the person or company you are negotiating with. If you are already in your current job and want to enter into a contract or renew a contract, you can't look at what you would be earning if you were working somewhere else. (If that is your goal, then go work somewhere else.)

Instead, ***do your homework*** and find out how others are being compensated in similar positions at your place of business, and more importantly, how a new lateral hire coming into a similar position is being compensated. It may be that base pay is pretty similar across the board, but the timing of the payments, the determination of the bonus, and the additional perks all may vary significantly.

Ask the open questions in your research: What are the available benefits and who has them? Is there anything else I should be considering? Are there benefits I am unaware of? Is there flexibility on the timing of the payments?

Get Help from Experts

Spend some significant time figuring out what you want to negotiate for and prioritizing it. In doing this research, women might want to ask men what they think. Developing a "kitchen cabinet" of successful men and women will be invaluable.

It is also important to hire an attorney and an accountant who are well versed in the legal and economic terms in contracts for similar persons in your field, and are therefore aware of the different types of clauses that would go into those types of contracts, as well as the ranges of ballpark fees. That research will help you determine how you want to negotiate.

Plan ahead in establishing value

About fifteen years ago I was involved with a client in the negotiation of a major league sports team. The agent who was instrumental in the deal told me a very valuable piece of advice. He said,

> *"When you are entering a contract, you have to set the value at the beginning. You only make big money twice – when you enter a contract and when you leave. All in the middle is just maintenance."*

I have thought about that advice a lot. You cannot enter into a contract for $150,000 a year and then think that you will be able to **earn your way up** to $250,000 a year. You set the value proposition at $150,000 and unless that additional $100,000 or the mechanism for obtaining it is somehow built into that initial contract, no employer or business colleague is going to decide that you are worth the extra $100,000 unless you are bringing a very significant increase in value to the table, which is unlikely.

All contracts can be renegotiated and amended. **The signing of a contract is a beginning point,** not the end. For that reason, you may wish to consider the length of the contract. My feeling is that most contracts should be of three year duration – especially if they are for significant sums. That is because it takes a least a year to figure out how to achieve results and get established, a year to show your performance, and another year to renegotiate the contract for better terms.

Bonnie Brown Hartley, a successful family business consultant says, "When trying to determine fees for a project, remember that if you undercharge initially you will ultimately either lose money or resent the contract."

Doing Your Homework

Find out the range of fees others in your field charge. Create a spreadsheet of all known expenses, including your time. Consider any work-related travel time, too. You don't need to add it, but you should understand the value of your time and the cost of travel if you choose not to charge for it.

You may feel shy about negotiating for yourself or uncomfortable about being your own advocate, but there is simply no other course. Learning to overcome the shyness and discomfort is something you really need to do. Once you have done the research, you'll know the terms and conditions that are right for you when setting the stage for this phase of your life. *Start advocating for yourself now.*

Create your own review

This is also true in your existing job/career. In most positions as an employee you are "reviewed" on an annual basis. That is when you are called in and your strengths, weaknesses, and areas of improvement are summarized. Often this review is tied to your compensation/ bonus/career track. Many people make this a one-way process. They expect to be judged, and they listen to what is said.

A better idea is to take the time in advance to **review all your accomplishments and write them down.** After all, who knows better than you what you are doing and what value you bring to the organization?

In one of my first associate positions, I was pretty sure no one understood what I had accomplished. When I knew that I was going to be reviewed, I put together a ten-page report on what I had done. The report was not just a list. It had numbers in it - ways that my results had driven revenue, client relationships that I had personally strengthened, and ideas and directions I had suggested. It also included a list of new ideas and strategies that I was currently working on. I knew what was important to the firm, and I made sure that my report addressed all of those factors and my contributions, and that it featured measurable results.

Impressive Results

The managing partner and committee were taken aback by the amount of work I had put into it. They told me they had never seen anything like that. At the end of the report I asked for a certain dollar bonus, *and I received it.* I later found out that the bonus I asked for was the highest bonus given to any associate that year.

Setting and achieving goals may be difficult to do on your own. Sometimes the right thing to do is to hire a coach. As executive coach Cynthia Adams Harrison of Thomas Davidow & Associates notes, just like athletic coaches, the goal of executive coaches is to enhance performance by identifying and limiting both internal and external distractions.

Internal distractions are those which come from within the individual, such as lack of confidence, negative thinking and anxiety - either self imposed, or aggravated by increased pressure for job performance. External business distractions come from the environment and are primarily related to industry and corporate limits. They can include a noisy work place, unexpected events, a lack of financial, technical or personnel resources, a hostile or non-communicative manager, compensatory practices, organizational constructs/designs, the cultural and political environment, and goal orientation. Good executive coaches develop an understanding of the system you are working in and then create interventions which will help you achieve your goals.

When you are able to achieve your goals, you'll find it easier to ask for the compensation you deserve. Remember to always negotiate a contract; getting your agreement in writing will help you to focus on your work. Consider the market and your industry, do your homework, ask for what you believe you are worth and then bring it to the table.

 Brian Tracy has started, built, managed, or turned around twenty-two businesses and has consulted for more than 1,000 businesses worldwide. He is president of Business Growth Strategies, an Internet-based program teaching business, sales, and entrepreneurship worldwide.

He is also chairman and CEO of Brian Tracy International, a company specializing in the training and development of individuals and organizations. He has written more than forty books on personal and business success that have been translated into thirty-four languages. He has written and produced more than 300 audio and video learning programs.

Brian speaks on the subjects of personal and professional development to corporate and public audiences, including the executives and staffs of many of America's largest corporations. His exciting talks and seminars on leadership, selling, self-esteem, goals, strategy, creativity, and success psychology bring about immediate changes and long-term results. For more information, please visit:

Website: www.BrianTracy.com
E-mail: mschiller@briantracy.com

Chapter Six

This Too Shall Pass

Brian Tracy

Editor's Note: Just around the time I was pulling together all of the wonderful chapters for this very special anthology, Brian Tracy – who has been in ALL of **"The Power of the Platform"** *books – received some life-changing news. This inspiring chapter is taken from his blog entries of April, 2010.*

April 4, 2010 - The greatest blessing that we can have is ideal health, energy, and fitness. Unfortunately, health is something that we often do not think a lot about until we have health problems.

Over the past few weeks, starting with a regular medical checkup, the doctors discovered that I have a cancerous tumor in my throat that is fairly well along in development.

What a shock! My life was moving along quite smoothly, my physical health was great overall, new opportunities and possibilities were poking up all around me, and my attention was definitely elsewhere.

Now, I have to slam on the brakes, call a "time out," and redirect the entire focus of my life toward my health and survival. What a bummer!

Since this cancer occurred, I began researching my situation. I have met a lot of wonderful and skilled people who work in the world of cancer treatment. It seems that there are millions of people who experience cancer at some time in their lives, and then go through various combinations of surgery, chemotherapy, and radiation to deal with it.

It occurred to me that cancer can be a metaphor for any unexpected setback or reversal in life, especially in the areas of money, business, career, and marriage. In each case, when your situation abruptly changes for the worse, you go through a process of shock and denial, followed by depression and self-pity, which is then followed by acceptance and resurgence.

Perhaps the most important four words in the English language, words that are always true for all people at all times are, ***"This too shall pass."***

William James of Harvard once wrote, "The first step in dealing with any problem is to be willing to have it so."

Primary Factors of Unhappiness

The primary factors that cause unhappiness come from stress and frustration, and most of the negative emotions are attachment and resistance. When you become attached to a particular outcome and you don't get that outcome or you get something else, you can become angry, frustrated, and resentful. This is why Buddha built much of his religion around the importance of "non-attachment," which requires that you simply let go of your attachment to a particular outcome and just allow the world and the situation to unfold in its own time and in its own way.

Jesus taught the principle of "non-resistance." He said "resist not evil." What this means is that it is the resistance to a particular situation or outcome that causes the stress, not the situation itself.

In dealing with my cancer, or with any other unexpected problem, reversal, or crisis, my first course of action is to remain calm, detached from the results or situation, and to simply accept that "what ever it is, it is."

There is a direct relationship between optimism and the strength of your immune system. There is a direct relationship between the strength of your immune system and your body's ability to combat cancer or any other physical problem.

Optimism Mechanism #1

The way that you remain optimistic is to deliberately look for something good in the situation, something that you may not have seen or thought about. Maybe it is a chance to change your career, relationships, or lifestyle. You may have been meaning to do one of these things for a long time anyway. Now is your chance.

Optimism Mechanism #2

The second way to remain optimistic is to seek the valuable lesson in whatever has occurred.

Maybe you have been trying too hard, or doing something that was wrong for you. Maybe you have been harboring negative emotions or grudges from past experiences that have depressed your immune system and made you more susceptible to physical ailments. Maybe the lesson is that you need to be focused on what is truly important in your life.

My battle with cancer has just begun. It is going to be an unpleasant experience involving considerable pain, distress, and severe weight loss. It is not something that anyone looks forward to.

But "what cannot be cured must be endured." In the weeks ahead, I will keep you informed of my progress and the situation as it unfolds. I have full confidence in a complete cure. I am positive, optimistic, and cheerful. I refuse to allow this situation to get me down. For each of you who may be going through your own "dark night of the soul," remember to look for the good, seek the valuable lesson, and tell yourself that "this too shall pass."

UPDATE: I began chemo yesterday, Thursday, April 15. I will soon learn how I respond physically and then be able to plan my life and work around it.

When you think about it, having cancer can be a metaphor for any big problem or unexpected setback in life. It happens unexpectedly, like job loss, bankruptcy, or divorce. You react with surprise, shock, and dismay. Then, you finally accept "the facts on the ground."

From that point onward, the only thing that matters is how you deal with it. Do you accept the new reality and get busy doing what is in your power to do, or do you become angry or depressed and blame other people or circumstances?

I choose to see this as a "learning experience." Maybe I'll develop a speech or seminar to share what I've learned and its parallels with the ups and down of normal life.

Fortunately, the doctor tells me that I am "asymptomatic," which means that I have NO symptoms aside from an irritation in my throat. This is good news.

I have confirmed my speaking schedule to all of my clients, right up to May 29 in Vienna, Austria, right after three days in London. I'll probably need a rest!

One fact has jumped out at me (again) during this process and that is the incredible excellence of the American medical system. The quality and dedication of the doctors and nurses is wonderful - very reassuring.

More good news! The success/survival rate of my type of cancer is 90% or more. My intention is to raise that average with excellent nutrition and proper care.

Brian, your family of friends at The Las Vegas Convention Speakers Bureau and around the world wish you a swift recovery. You'll be in our hearts and in our prayers.

Arielle believes that finding true love is possible for anyone, at any age, and she points to herself as living proof – having married for the first time at age 44. She expanded the same set of business skills that she used to launch her highly successful Public Relations firm, The Ford Group, and applied them to her love life.

Arielle is best known for helping to launch the careers of many bestselling self-help and spiritual authors including Deepak Chopra, Jack Canfield and Mark Victor Hansen – co-creators of **Chicken Soup for the Soul**, Neale Donald Walsh, and many others.

As an author, Arielle has written seven books as of this printing, including the **Hot Chocolate for the Mystical Soul** series. Her latest book is **The Soulmate Secret: How To Manifest The Love of Your Life with the Law of Attraction**.

Arielle lives in La Jolla, California with her husband, Brian Hilliard, and their feline friends.

Website: *www.arielleford.com*
E-mail: *af@fordsisters.com*
Twitter: *@arielleford*
Facebook: *ariellefordfanpage*

Chapter Seven

Finding Big Love Is Possible At Any Age

Arielle Ford

Is it your dream to find a soul mate....a life-partner who will love, cherish and adore you? I didn't meet and marry my soul mate until I was forty-four. I learned a lot along the way about what does and doesn't work in the world of love and romance.

Here's what I know for sure: finding true love is possible for any one at *any* age if you're willing to prepare yourself, on all levels, to become a magnet for love.

This wonderful Universe of ours is set up to deliver the people and things we draw to us that are consistent with our personal belief system. If you don't believe you will ever find "the ONE" then, guess what? You get to be right; you probably won't.

If, however, you learn to believe that the ONE is not only out there but is ALSO LOOKING FOR YOU, then true love can be yours.

When I was in my early forties I decided to manifest my soul mate using everything I had ever learned about manifestation, psychology, spirituality, and the Law of Attraction. My intentions became crystal clear while I simultaneously cleared out the clutter in my house AND in my heart. I learned and invented techniques, rituals, visualizations and prayers that helped me prepare my body, mind, spirit, and home for an amazing relationship. It worked; I met my husband, Brian, who has exceeded all of my desires and expectations.

It's not your job to know HOW your soul mate is going to appear, only to be ready, willing, and OPEN to love. Love has always been there for you; you just need to remember the love that you *are.* Once you do, the Universe will deliver to you the perfect soul mate.

The basic Law of Attraction states that you will attract to you those things that match your state of belief. If we believe the world is a loving and friendly place, then most of the time, that will be our experience. But, if we believe the world is a chaotic, stressful and fearful place, then that becomes our reality. So, believing and knowing that your soul mate is out there is critical to the preparation of manifestation.

Prior to meeting Brian thirteen years ago, I had a daily ritual in which I would light several candles at sunset, put on my favorite CD of Gregorian chants and sit in my big, cozy chair. With my eyes closed I would drop into the feeling of remembering the joy of having my soul mate in my life. I would experience these wonderful feelings in every part of my body, feeling and knowing that his arrival was assured.

Here are the top ten things to do in order to manifest your soul mate:

- Be the loving person that you are. Find ways to express more love to everyone in your life.

- Live in the knowingness that you are in a loving, committed relationship.

- Live that truth every day as you savor the waiting for your beloved to arrive.

- Create a "treasure map" of your romantic vision and look at it daily.

- Write a list of the most important qualities your soul mate will possess.

- Heal your heart of any past hurts that will prevent you from magnetizing big love.

- Clear out the clutter in your closets and home; create space for your beloved.

- Create an altar in the relationship corner of your home.

- Listen to your intuition; take action when opportunities present themselves.

- Fall in love with yourself. Know that you are loveable.

Big love is possible for any one at any age. Become a magnet for love. Live each day in the knowingness that you are in a loving, committed relationship as you enjoy waiting for your beloved to arrive.

Cammy Dierking is a highly sought-after motivational speaker who projects a contagious and wild enthusiasm for everything she does. Her messages are thoughtful, clear, uplifting, and presented in an energetic and lively way that's chockfull of laughs! Her achievement of finishing an **IRONMAN** triathlon inspires audiences everywhere.

Cammy enjoys a career in TV Broadcasting that spans thirty years. Currently the Evening News Anchor at the CBS affiliate in Cincinnati, Ohio, Cammy began her TV career as a Sportscaster.

Inspired by her father, Connie Dierking, a former NBA Basketball Player, Cammy was one of the first female TV Sports Anchors in the country, and was THE first in the state of Ohio. Cammy's popular topics include attitude, balance, and living your dream.

Website: www.cammydierking.com
E-mail: info@cammydierking.com

Chapter Eight

Boost Your Karma

Cammy Dierking

I held my Mom's hand as she lay in the bed at hospice. I talked to her constantly, assuring her that she wasn't alone, and that I loved her ...forever. I placed her hand on my pregnant belly and promised her that I would tell her grandchild what an incredible mother she was and what an incredible grandmother she would have been. Her breathing was shallow and sporadic. And then...there were no more breaths. I lost my dear, sweet, wonderful Mom. She was only 50. She missed the birth of her first grandchild by just two weeks.

Mom's death left a huge, gaping hole in my heart. But that hole began to fill back up with hope and love when I gave birth to my beautiful daughter, Kylee. She was a healthy, adorable bundle of pure joy. She had a full head of light brown hair, big blue eyes, and chubby pink cheeks. Kylee became my reason for living ... the air in my lungs.

More Changes

By the time Kylee was three months old, she would smile when I rubbed noses with her or when she heard her Daddy's voice. One

Saturday morning, my husband and I woke up and whispered our excitement to one another... we thought our baby had finally slept through the night! When John went to check on her, he let out a blood-curdling scream. Kylee was dead in her crib. Our perfect little angel had died of Sudden Infant Death Syndrome.

The hole in my heart opened up again and this time, it threatened to swallow me. I went to a very dark and depressing place. There were times I wondered if I would ever smile or feel happy again. With the help of my family and friends, I was able to slowly crawl out of that hole (although some days I slid back in, just a little.) But what truly got me back to the surface, and what sustains me every day, is the belief that things can and will get better. I know that in life there will be disappointment and heartache; it's a given. What's not a given is how we choose to get through it all. If we look hard enough, we can always find the bright side. It's a realization that changed my life - and it can change yours.

From Tragedy to Triumph

We travel in search of it, marry for the sake of it, see therapists to enhance it, or switch jobs to capture it. Yet for many, happiness remains elusive. The GREAT news is that we can create our own happy reality - right now! We can transition from those dark places to happiness by changing our choices, attitudes, and thoughts.

C'mon...get happy! Here are some ideas and proven techniques to help you regain and maintain a sense of joy:

1. **C'mon Get Moving!** Exercise improves your self-image, mood, and outlook. A regular exercise program (filled with fun activities) combined with a healthy diet (like avoiding processed foods) and plenty of sleep is a powerful recipe for cooking up lifelong joy and satisfaction!

2. **C'mon Get Smart!** Train your brain to challenge negative thoughts, and ALWAYS look for the positive in every situation. (Losing a child was devastating, but it makes me truly appreciate my three daughters every day. And I NEVER take their health for granted.) Develop a hopeful mantra to get you through anxious moments - for instance, always tell yourself "Everything is an opportunity."

3. **C'mon Get Connected!** People whose lives are enriched by strong friendships and loving relationships feel more satisfied, secure, and content. Happiness is contagious, so spend time with upbeat people and stay away from negative people; they are "emotional vampires" because they suck the life out of you!

4. **C'mon Get Thankful!** An attitude of gratitude ups our happiness level by helping us appreciate the present moment and all the wonderful people and things in our lives.

Giving thanks allows us to let go of anger, old grudges, and negative emotions.

5. C'mon Get Altruistic! This one is simple: Do good, feel good. When you are compassionate, generous, and kind to others, it lowers your stress level, enhances your own health and well-being, and generates pleasurable emotions.

Boost Your Karma!

Let's take this altruism thing a step further. There's a cosmic principle called "KARMA." The thinking is that if you do good things, good things will happen to you. Conversely, if you do bad things, bad things will happen to you. (This is an oversimplification, but you get the idea!) Karma essentially means you don't get away with anything!

Attitudes and thoughts can also provoke good or bad karma. Here's how: attitudes shape our expectations; when we expect something to happen, we consciously or subconsciously take actions to make it happen. This means that if you think positive thoughts, you'll attract health, wealth, and happiness. Think negative thoughts and you'll attract poverty, illness, and loneliness.

Try These Tips

Here are some tips for shifting your thoughts toward the positive to create a successful and incredible life (ie. boosting your karma):

1. **Declare!** Be clear in your mind about the good things you want to happen. Tell your friends and loved ones what you plan to accomplish. Visualize yourself being successful every step of the way.

2. **Believe!** Have unwavering faith that you WILL reach your goals. Keep in mind that negative events are temporary. Remember - life is full of promise!

3. **Share!** When you succeed, you feel good. When you feel good, you radiate enthusiasm and energy, and that is contagious. Have a winning attitude, share your exuberance, and celebrate your successes with the important people in your life!

The Proof Is In The ("Karma-Lized") Pudding

How do I know these methods really work? I have tried and tested them. In fact, it is how I live my life every day. Here is the best example of a time in my life when employing these karma-boosting techniques enabled me to achieve a lifelong dream:

Dreaming of an Ironman

I was very athletic when I was younger, and I always dreamed of competing in an Ironman Triathlon (2.4 mile swim; 112 mile bike ride; 26.2 mile run.) However, I grew up with juvenile rheumatoid arthritis. After more than a dozen surgeries to stabilize my joints, I finally needed a total knee replacement at age 45. Common sense might suggest that competing in an Ironman was now out of the question, but I was not about to abandon my dream.

I had seen triathletes with only one leg or with other serious physical limitations compete in the Hawaiian Ironman Championships; if they could do it, so could I!

The Dream Begins

A year after my replacement, I told my family and friends that I intended to FINISH an Ironman Triathlon. I signed up for Ironman Louisville (**Declare!**). Training was time-consuming and challenging, but I gained confidence with every stroke, every revolution, and every mile.

I often thought about how fortunate I was to have the physical and mental strength to endure the sometimes grueling workouts. I realized that during the race, I would have to swim and bike as FAST as possible so that I'd save enough time to walk the marathon (I couldn't run because of the intense pain in my joints.) I decided that quitting was NOT an option and that I WOULD cross the finish line under the 17-hour time limit (**Believe!**).

The day I competed in Ironman was one of the BEST days of my life! Yes, it was a long day with some tough moments, but I was so happy to be there chasing my dream that I smiled through the entire race. I enjoyed the beauty of the Kentucky horse farms, encouraged the other triathletes, and thanked all the volunteers and fans along the course. At the finish line, I felt like a rock star! With a spotlight on me (it was late at night at that point!) and thousands of people cheering, I limped toward the red carpet along the finishing chute. My family was waiting for me at the finish line, and my three daughters and I clasped hands and ran across together (**Share!**). We were screaming and laughing and crying, and I'll always remember how exciting and overwhelming the experience was. I heard the announcer shout: "Cammy Dierking, you are an Ironman!" I finished the race in 15 hours and 40 minutes. It was an AMAZING adventure!

I am convinced that a chain reaction of positive thoughts and positive actions led me to such a positive outcome. In other words, great KARMA got me across the Ironman finish line. If I could do that, just imagine what a little positive karma could do for you!!!

Tom Stone is an expert in developing new techniques for resolving trauma and anxiety. As founder and CEO of **Great Life Technologies, Inc.,** he provides trauma and anxiety resolution services for veterans, active duty military personnel and their families.

Tom studied at the San Francisco Conservatory of Music where he developed a strong interest in the physics of music. This later served as the perfect background for the study of biophysics-based healing concepts.

He has a deep understanding of addiction recovery and is a leading teacher of applied kinesiology. Tom is a popular speaker throughout the world and is the author of four books, including *"The Power of How," "Pure Awareness,"* and *"Vaporize Your Anxiety."* Discover more about Tom at:

Websites:	*www.greatlifetechnologies.com*
	www.vaporizeyouranxiety.com
Facebook:	*tomstoneglt*
Twitter:	*@tomstoneglt*
LinkedIn:	*TomStone*
Phone:	*888-928-3625*

Chapter Nine

Vaporize Your Traumas & Anxieties

Tom Stone

One of the most important things you can do to have a great life is clean up your inner emotional landscape. ***Unresolved emotional pain is the result of very early, in fact preverbal childhood conditioning.*** Everyone has emotionally overwhelming experiences when they are very young.

I've yet to meet anyone who liked such experiences. To avoid feeling overwhelmed, we tend to put a lid on our natural ability to feel things. We prefer to limit our access to those emotional traumas. The result is trapped emotional energy in our bodies, and the accumulation of a big database of unresolved emotional pain.

Unresolved traumas = problems in your life

These unresolved traumas are the basis of just about every problem in human life. They are the underpinnings of anxiety, depression, addictions, suicidal tendencies, and post traumatic stress disorder.

Scientific research has now proven that traumas also crystallize into physical illness as spelled out by Dr. Vincent Felitti in his article on the ACE Study: "The Relation Between Adverse Childhood Experiences and Adult Health." Even if you don't suffer from such problems, your personal database of unresolved emotional pain still profoundly limits your ability to succeed and enjoy life.

I know first-hand the damage that can result from experiencing trauma, and the challenges associated with understanding and overcoming it. On December 7th, 1993, a deranged stranger wielding a .44 caliber handgun shot me in the chest. My survival was nothing short of miraculous.

Understandably, the resulting trauma of this assault motivated me to search for **real solutions and methods** to resolve not just what had happened to me, but **to help anyone** who has had a traumatic experience.

This quest led me to the forefront of discovering techniques that are now being used to train Trauma Resolution Specialists world-wide. Beyond veterans and active duty military personnel, these techniques have been found to be equally effective in helping victims of rape, violent crime, and domestic abuse. They have also been used by first responders, especially in natural disasters.

New, powerful techniques

Until now, these problems had been difficult - if not impossible - to solve. Again, most people are simply not good at moving past the residue of emotional pain from traumatic energy and instead trap it in the body, which leads to the problems mentioned earlier. But recent major breakthroughs are changing all of this.

In my book, *"Vaporize Your Anxiety without Drugs or Therapy,"* I describe some completely new and very powerful techniques. These methods reveal ways for us to do the exact opposite of what we are deeply conditioned to do. Instead of going away from the intense center of emotional pain, you discover how to dive right into it. By thoroughly experiencing and processing the essence of the pain, it is dissolved and there is nothing left to feel.

It turns out that the most intense center of the energy field of the emotion is similar to an **"eye of the hurricane"** type of vortex. By bravely going to the center of that vortex, you can complete the incomplete experience that is held there – very quickly and thoroughly. To a three-year-old child, this would be a terrifying prospect. But, for the adult in us, the process of re-experiencing the core of our emotional overwhelm is easier than we may have thought.

The technique described above is called the **CORE Technique**. CORE is an acronym for **Center of Remaining Energy,** which describes the technique beautifully. I train the Trauma Resolution Specialists to use the CORE Technique to resolve Combat Stress (also know as *Post Traumatic Stress Disorder or PTSD*) in veterans of the Vietnam, Iraq and Afghanistan Wars. Our success is *mind-blowing.*

Vaporizing PTSD

Many of the Vietnam War vets I worked with hadn't had a good night's sleep in over forty years, often waking from nightmares. *This was true even for vets who had been in traditional therapy for fifteen years.* In each case, I used the CORE Technique to resolve the traumas that were causing the nightmares, thereby allowing these veterans to sleep through the night for eight or nine hours – *beginning that very night* – without a single nightmare. And the good sleep has continued ever since.

The CORE Technique is just one of eight techniques for resolving trauma and anxiety. These new techniques are called the **Pure Awareness Techniques**. They guide the person to both resolve the energy of the traumatic or anxious feelings, which results in their being able to attain a peaceful state: the experience of one's own awareness.

Dr. Michael Telch, Founder of the Laboratory for the Study of Anxiety Disorders at the University of Texas, Austin, is directing a study to determine the impact that the Pure Awareness Techniques can have on anxiety. A survey designed by Dr. Telch is being used to determine just how much we can reduce the symptoms of PTSD using these techniques. **This is great news for veterans and others who suffer from PTSD.**

Veterans are amazed at the results

Ken Strickland, a retired Sergeant Major in the United States Marine Corps, was in the service for twenty-six years. After experiencing the CORE technique, he recommended that the treatment **not be limited to returning soldiers, but also expanded to include active duty soldiers.** He found the results to be that powerful.

About seventeen years ago, Vietnam veteran and Purple Heart recipient Ernie D'Leon, was diagnosed with PTSD. He hadn't been able to sleep *"like a normal person"* for more than 40 years. He suffered from nightmares and hyper-vigilance; any noise, light, or other change would wake him up and it was difficult for him to get back to sleep.

Ernie had been through **seventeen years of therapy**. The reality was that he did not want to live with PTSD all his life, so he was always looking for an answer.

Ernie says he was amazed and enthralled when he heard about my work. I asked him how he would like to sleep for eight straight hours. He was eager to try this. After his first session, he smiled broadly and later he told me, *"I slept nine hours that night."*

Debugging our Lives

In essence, Pure Awareness Techniques are a lot like **debugging and upgrading your Inner Human Software.** If your computer isn't giving you the desired output, you may have "software issues" that need to be addressed. It's really not that much different for us. Our Inner Human

Software™ is made up of our thoughts, feelings, and intentions. These control our "output."

Human Software Engineering (HSE) is a revolutionary way of finding and fixing the causes of problems in human life. We use a computer software analogy because **computers were modeled after humans,** so computer hardware and software concepts can help us easily understand how we as humans actually work.

These techniques, however, are not just for people with extreme anxiety and trauma such as veterans or victims of serious crimes. They are useful to everyone as *a new way to remove the inner causes of problems*, suffering, and limitations. In many instances, people have been searching for the kind of results that these Pure Awareness Techniques deliver, but – until now – have not had significant results.

A client of mine shared that she had dealt with anxiety and codependency issues that had haunted her all of her life. She had experienced modest results with cognitive therapy as well as EFT techniques, but our system of "debugging and upgrading one's inner human software" had a dramatically deeper and longer lasting effect. Her original hope of experiencing just one week free of anxiety has now turned into months of feeling anxiety-free.

For many of us **limitations have become routine,** and a part of life we tolerate no matter how much it holds us back and keeps us from enjoying the life we really want. *It is no longer* *necessary to continue to be the victim of your emotions.*

Technique Meets Technology

We now have an **interactive iPhone application** that can guide you through the Pure Awareness Techniques while your eyes are closed. You simply touch a big button on the screen of the iPhone when you are ready for the next audio instruction. You can find a link to this iPhone app, along with more information about the Pure Awareness Techniques, by visiting www.VaporizeYourAnxiety.com. These new techniques can help you to improve your personal life by dramatically *reducing stress, anxiety and trauma.*

Imagine helping others

On the site you'll also find information about new career opportunities. You can learn how to help people resolve their trauma and anxiety, learn to be a trainer or coach using these techniques, or even come to work for **Great Life Technologies, Inc**. If you've never seen anyone heal in a matter of minutes, I invite you to find out more about these fascinating breakthrough techniques, as well as listen to and watch demonstrations of the techniques in progress at www.VaporizeYourCombatStress. com. It will change the way you think about trauma and help you to understand that you can resolve such problems now much more easily and thoroughly than ever before, as you strive towards living a great life.

Roshini Rajkumar guides C-level executives, authors, athletes, and politicos to powerful media and industry performances. Her background makes her a popular contributing expert with local and national media. In her first book, **"*Communicate That!*"**, she shares insider tips for dynamic communication and impressive presentations.

Roshini is a former television broadcaster. In that role, she launched an investigative unit, hosted TV and radio talk shows, and reported and anchored the news. She won the Edward R. Murrow Award for team coverage of the 2008 Republican National Convention Riot for CBS Radio Minneapolis.

Roshini delivers her unique style as an emcee for special events, a radio host, and as commercial talent. She is a guest professor at St. Catherine University.

Websites: *www.roshinimedia.com*
www.communicatethatbook.com
E-mail: *roshini@roshinimedia.com*
Facebook: *roshini.rajkumar*
Twitter: *@RoshiniR*
Phone: *612-910-0826*

Chapter Ten

Life—It Is Really Quite Simple

Roshini Rajkumar

"Life is as difficult or as simple as you make it." When I say this to friends and clients, I get several different reactions. Some take it with suspicion, as if they couldn't possibly be responsible for making their own lives any easier. For others, it comes as an "ah-ha moment" and becomes a license for self-empowerment.

My simple statement is a call to action; it is, in essence, a road map for helping you find the biggest thrills and highest levels of fulfillment, all while keeping life simple and enjoyable. Feel your *passion*, discover your sense of *mission*, and enjoy each day for all of the *fun* it can bring.

Feel Your Passion

When I began as a news reporter in 1998, I could never have imagined exactly how the events in my life would lead me to a career as a professional speaker and to the publication of my first book, *"Communicate That!"* What I did know, however, was that my *passion* was for news, people, and good storytelling through powerful words and images.

Being able to communicate effectively can improve your circumstances and help you achieve greater success in business and in life. Imagine being able to close more deals, enjoy greater confidence, build better relationships, or even convince your family to order take-out instead of cooking dinner on those nights when you're tired!

This passion for excellence in communication became my driving force. As a reporter, I woke up every morning looking for interesting people with unique stories. It was my job to bring their triumphs and tribulations to the masses. My passion was *fueled* every time I met extraordinary characters.

Inspiring Characters

One such impressive story centered around 2-year-old Caleb in Des Moines, Iowa. You'll find out why his fatherless status inspired others to step up. His father's fraternity brothers were helping to raise Caleb in their fraternity house so his mother could finish school at Iowa State University. Everyone was working together to help the young family have a better life, in spite of the tragic death of Caleb's father in an icy road accident when Caleb was just a baby.

My sense of passion as a journalist was *inspired* by musicians, politicians, and people from all walks who were at the top of their game. As a rookie reporter, I interviewed Garth Brooks in Fargo, North Dakota. Years later, I interviewed Patti LaBelle in Detroit. Even as a more seasoned journalist, I was awe-struck by this musical icon.

I interviewed Al Gore when he was on the presidential campaign trail. I had the chance to interview Elizabeth Dole before the Iowa Straw Poll of 1999. The results of that poll led to her eventual departure from her quest for the country's highest office.

I conducted exclusive interviews with national sports figures including the Tennessee Titan's Eddie George, Kevin Garnett when he was with the Minnesota Timberwolves just before he won the MVP Award, and "Big Boss Man," a pro wrestler on the Raw Tour. Studying these "greats" through interviewing them helped me connect *powerful performance* with *power to shape* one's destiny.

Discover Your Mission

Passion ignites us, but a sense of mission about our destiny enables us to share that passion with a world yearning for inspiration. As a newswoman, I got to deliver amazing stories – I was a witness to history. This planted the seeds for realizing the true mission of my work – to help people understand how effective communication is the great differentiator that leads to success.

Dynamically sharing and illuminating one's own stories of passion can help anyone rise to great heights in business, life, and spirit.

I could not have done justice to Caleb, his mother, or the young men in the fraternity if I had not been able to shine light on their story. After I left the Des Moines TV market for Nashville, I learned that the fraternity brothers had been recognized by the governor for their outstanding citizenry. I smile when I think about them all and wonder what Caleb is up to now. He may never realize how he touched my life, but I am happy to have helped bring his story into the public eye.

Sharing stories with integrity and authenticity became the brand for my mission. Indeed, it became my communication style. I soon realized, however, that the life of a TV reporter can weigh on one's heart. We cover the best of life, like WWII veterans gathering to celebrate one another on the 60th anniversary of the end of the war. We also cover the worst of life, like the Space Shuttle Columbia disintegrating upon re-entry to Earth in February, 2003.

A good journalist develops a shield of sorts, so that he or she can do the job from as objective a place possible and effectively communicate the facts to viewers.

Do you have a sense of purpose in your life – something that drives you to embrace each day with a burning passion? Then you have found your mission, and you should enthusiastically pursue it. If not, think about what gets you excited and discover more about it until you **connect with it so deeply** that it becomes your mission.

Don't Forget the Fun!

Along with passion and a sense of mission, it's important to remember to have fun along the way. The nature of my work as a journalist was often serious or centered on life-altering circumstances and human drama. Thankfully, I was raised by parents who celebrated life and focused on life's positive aspects. The contrast between how I was raised and where my work took me made it apparent that **having fun is critical to keeping life simple and enjoyable**.

Fun fuels my passion and keeps my mission fresh and moving forward. Make sure that you take time to have fun each day. You'll see how focusing on the lighter aspects of life will lift you up. I know you'll start to appreciate everything else in your life more, too. If days pass without a laugh or without moments of pure joy, make a dedicated effort to spend quality time with friends, see a movie, or do something that will break your cycle. You owe it to yourself AND your mission to *take a moment for fun every day*.

Helping Others to Become Better Communicators

My mission has evolved to a point where I now focus on helping others communicate powerfully within the business world – through keynote speaking, through coaching executive clients on their presentation skills, and through my writing. It is my desire that people discover the importance of becoming powerful communicators, and that they **develop the**

skills necessary to deliver their thoughts and ideas effectively. It's disturbing to me to see intelligent, talented people fail to express themselves well.

Everyone has the capacity to improve his or her communication skills. By becoming more aware of what you are saying and how you are saying it and by being willing to put forth the effort necessary to improve your communication techniques, you can avoid misunderstandings, share greater compassion, and *become more skilled at communicating important thoughts and messages.*

A Simple Formula to Help

I am so passionate about this mission that I developed and trademarked a presentation process. I call it the **I-A-P™ Formula**. IAP stands for **Intent-Audience Analysis-Powerful Performance**. Using this formula, I teach people how to simplify their communication preparation and delivery process. When you keep the preparation simple, powerful performance will come easily. *The ability to communicate effectively and present your authentic self will help you feel greater self-confidence as you engage your passion.*

Fun, then, becomes a natural byproduct, if not a direct goal you set for yourself or your audience. I know I could not stay focused or energized on my mission without having fun ***EVERY DAY!*** Take time for family dinners, golf with friends, or lunch with a favorite client.

Simple pleasures can bring much-needed fun that will help to keep you healthy, sane, and passionate. No matter how busy you are, there is always time for fun. Laughter and positive energy will actually help you to focus when you are under pressure or in pursuit of your mission. *Take your work seriously, but not yourself.*

I am in a good place – I'm on a mission, and I am engaging my passion. As a result, ***I never really feel like I'm working***. My work is rewarding and my communication style has evolved to a point where it delivers a tremendous sense of fun for me.

Rather than worry about life or how to get from "Point A to Point B" or beyond, try passionately living your mission without overlooking the simple things or the fun that pursuing your passion can provide. When you're on the right path, it's really that simple!

Chuck Bolton is a C-level executive coach, retained by CEOs and senior executives who seek positive change in their leaders and top teams through behavioral coaching. Chuck is the developer of **Top Team Check**, a proprietary team assessment tool and has assessed more than 100 top teams in the US, Canada, Europe and Israel.

Chuck is the author of **Leadership Wipeout: The Story of an Executive's Crash and Rescue, The Dirtiest Little Secret in Business: The Absence of Supportive Candor** and the soon to be released **The Hole in Your Team.**

Chuck frequently speaks on leadership topics for corporations, associations, universities, and non-profits. He has appeared as an expert source in the national media including CBS, NBC and FOX. For more information, visit Chuck at:

Chuck's site: www.chuckbolton.info
Company site: www.theboltongroup.com
E-mail: chuck@theboltongroup.com
LinkedIn: ChuckBolton
Twitter: @ChuckBolton
Facebook: chuckbolton
Phone: 800-310-9020

Chapter Eleven

The Hole in Your Team

Chuck Bolton

As the leader of a business, you depend on others to make things happen. Your "Top Team" helps run the show and get things done. On a scale of 1 (low) to 10 (high), how effective is your top team today?

If your business is like most, there's a hole in your top team. When performance leaks out, top teams fail to reach their potential. When you can fill the hole, your top team will gain alignment and finally be able to perform to its fullest ability.

The need for executive-level collaboration and optimal team performance has never been greater. Globalization, rapid innovation, and relentless competition require a cohesive and highly effective leadership response. Top teams drive the performance of a company and have a great impact on its market capitalization.

Senior leaders have little choice but to build high-performing, top leadership teams that will operate in extraordinary ways and contribute to company growth, while creating a positive working climate.

The Problem with Top Teams

Unfortunately, many top teams are often not teams at all, but rather a collection of ambitious, strong-minded executives who prefer to work individually - sometimes at cross purposes. Consider the following:

- Only 20 percent of CEOs rate their top teams "high-performing."

- When asked *"How effective is our top leadership team today on a scale of 1-10, and how effective should it be?"* CEOs responded 6.2 and 9.6, and their direct reports responded 5.9 and 9.4 respectively.

- Direct reports typically see a team's performance about 15 percent worse than the team leaders.

- Trust is an issue in over 65 percent of top teams.

What can be done to avoid that gap in team performance?

Getting Started

Top team leaders have the single biggest impact on the performance and dynamics of the team. They must answer these questions:

- Is there a need and desire to lift the company's performance?

- Am I willing to let the top team share in leading the company?

- Who should be on the top team?

- On what key areas should the top team focus its efforts and energies?

The Three Dimensions of Top Team Performance

There are three critical dimensions of top-team performance that, when aligned, lead to high performance. They are **creating clarity, building capabilities, and increasing commitment.**

Creating Clarity

Creating Clarity

Creating clarity means becoming crystal clear about the purpose, direction, and the desired results of the business and the top team. It addresses the norms of behavior, and how to share information, make decisions, and raise and resolve conflict.

Creating clarity requires the team leader to determine which issues will best be resolved by an individual or a small group of executives or require the focus of the top team as a whole. ***Not every issue is worth the entire top team's focus and attention.*** Some examples of top team initiatives include:

- Conducting talent reviews and succession plans,

- Doing due diligence on a potential acquisition or integrating one,

- Growing globally or entering a new market,

- Building organizational capability and overseeing performance, and

- Managing critical efforts

Building Capabilities

Building Capabilities

Top teams grow their capabilities and develop a rhythm over time, both as individual team members and as a team. Capability building includes developing the skill and will of each team member to talk straight, give and receive feedback and feedforward and collaborate collegially. In building individual and collective capabilities toward greater emotional intelligence, it is important to use positive styles of leadership and to create a resonant working climate.

Increasing Commitment

Increasing Commitment

As clarity is created and capabilities are increased, positive results are achieved. With this success, the team members increase their commitment to the team. Relationships between team members strengthen. Team members have "each others' backs" and take responsibility for the top team's success and on-going performance. A belief emerges that when it's time for the top team to work together, the team can and will operate in a way that will drive an outcome greater than what could be achieved by an individual team member or small working group. As commitment increases, trust builds. Trust allows for conflict to be brought to the surface to be resolved safely. Finally, high-performing top teams take the time to reflect, renew, and celebrate while preparing for new opportunities.

The Most Important Factor in Team Performance

The team leader's approach determines the difference between a high-performing top team, and a frustrating waste of time and executive energy. A team leader who can envision the benefit of important work that is done collaboratively and cooperatively is a must. The team leader must believe that many minds are better than one. It requires a team leader who stacks the deck for a great team performance by ensuring that the right conditions are in place. This offers greater probability that the group of direct reports will transform into an extraordinary top team and be sustainable.

Questions for the team leader to consider are:

- What would be the benefit of improving the alignment and performance of your top team?

- Is your top team truly a strategic asset, performing to its full potential? Is yours a team a competitor would want to compete against?

- How can you leverage the performance of your top team? What are the critical differences that are required for extraordinary performance from your top team? What's the "20" that gets the "80"?

Top Team Alignment

By creating clarity, building capabilities, and increasing commitment, the top team will become more cohesive and supportive, able to perform at a higher level, and will share similar expectations of high individual and team performance. An extraordinary top team is a catalyst for winning in any market, which can be a very powerful competitive advantage that cannot be duplicated.

Renee Kim came to the United States as a young teenager and, ever since, has been unstoppable. She is the president and founder of CLI Groups, Inc., a Convention, Leisure, & Incentive travel company.

More recently, Renee became a Nu Skin Distributor where she continues to break sales records. She enjoys discovering new opportunities and shares her tips for success with her teams. Renee's strength lies in her drive and her ability to overcome obstacles. She can light a fire under any sales team in any industry.

Renee is a graduate of the University of Southern California with a double major in Finance and Marketing. Her early work as a stock broker helped her to develop not just her people skills but also her dynamic sales skills platform.

Website: *www.cligroups.com*
E-mail: *rkim@cligroups.com*
Facebook: *Renee Kim*
LinkedIn: *Renee Kim*
Phone: *702-219-2628*

Chapter Twelve

The Power of a Decision

Renee Kim

I wasn't a terribly shy girl growing up in Korea, but all that was about to change! When my family moved to America, I was just fourteen years old. I did not know the English language or the American culture. I grew shy, intimidated, and ashamed of who I was. I began to doubt myself; I lacked the confidence necessary to make my own decisions and, as a result, typically did what other people thought was best for me.

I remember ordering, "Pizza and coke, please," for an entire semester in seventh grade because I couldn't say "hamburger" or "French fries" or any other menu item that was spelled with an "R", "L", or "F". There is no such sound in the Korean language! I was terrified that if I said something wrong, I might be asked a question that I would not be able to answer.

How Times have Changed!

Today, I can order French fries or anything else I want. I am no longer a shy, little teenager. I am a confident businesswoman who can strike up a conversation with anyone, anywhere.

I accept myself for who I am. It took me a long time to get here, and there were many obstacles that I had to conquer to become the person I am today, including learning how to make decisions based upon my own needs and desires.

Opportunities and Obstacles

Opportunities come our way all the time. Unfortunately, unexpected obstacles can come our way too. Being able to spot opportunities and weather obstacles can be the difference between achieving success and descending into failure.

The choices we make today will guarantee tomorrow's outcome. Sometimes, though, we let emotions like fear and uncertainty cloud our judgment and get in the way, and we make decisions using poor judgment.

The FIRST Life-Altering Decision

I always knew I was going to go to college. I lived in Las Vegas, Nevada and was attending Eldorado High School. I studied hard to prepare to go to a great college to "BE SOMEBODY!" I applied to several colleges and was excited that I had been accepted at several schools. I chose to attend the University of Southern California.

I was filled with anticipation and was looking forward to going away. Everything was going great and I felt like I was going to conquer the world. Then, in my senior year, I fell in love with a boy. It's funny...I can't even remember his name anymore! I thought he was "The ONE!"

You can probably imagine the scene at home when I told my mother, "Mom, I don't want to go to college. I want to get married instead." I was in LOVE! My mother begged me, threatened me, grounded me, cried, beat me, and literally did everything in her power to make me go to college. She made me think about my future and she finally, somehow, convinced me to go. Off I went to USC.

I cringe today when I think about what might have happened if I had stayed and not gone to college. This was the first decision I can attribute to for who I am today.

Every Day We Make Decisions

You want to make something of yourself. You want to succeed, make more money, be healthier, travel more, and share quality time with your family. You want to *enjoy your life more!*

Are the decisions you are making today going to move you to where you want to be? Before you know it, years can pass and you might find yourself exactly in the same place you are today. If you want to improve your life, you must first make a decision to change.

Seeking Approval

After I graduated from USC, I made a decision to become a stockbroker because I wanted my mom to be proud of me. I knew she would enjoy bragging to her friends that I was a stockbroker in Beverly Hills. Eight years later, on September 12th, 2001, the day after 9/11, I lost everything. I lost all of my savings and my clients. But the worst thing was that I lost hope and all motivation.

I had never liked being a broker. Whenever I heard someone say, "I love what I do," I wanted to strangle that person. I hated my work. I was the worst employee. But, I was too afraid to make any changes. I was too comfortable with what I knew, and I didn't like the uncertainty of doing anything unfamiliar.

I was at the end of my rope with the only career I'd ever known; I didn't know what to do or where to turn. I felt like a miserable failure, and I needed to make another huge decision to change my life.

Listening to my Heart...Finally

This time, I thought long and hard about what **I wanted**, not what other people wanted for me or wanted me to be. Unfortunately, up until this point I had spent my life trying to please everyone else. I had no idea of what I liked or wanted to do.

One thing was certain: living in Los Angeles was expensive. I could not keep up the life style I had enjoyed before; I was broke. I wanted to move back to Las Vegas, but I was hesitant. Moving back to Las Vegas would mean that I had failed. I didn't think I would be able to return, knowing what everyone would think of me.

That is when I realized that I was about to make a bad decision based on the wrong criteria again. I needed to make a decision based on what I wanted – NOT based upon what other people wanted for me or thought of me.

I made my decision to move back to Las Vegas because that is **what I wanted**. It made sense, considering the fact that I was broke and could live with my family. I still wasn't sure what I was going to do. I could decide that later.

I had resolved to never again put myself in a situation where I felt stuck and hated everything about my work. I did not want to ever take a job just as a way to pay my bills.

A New Opportunity

Once back in Las Vegas and working a regular "job," I found myself with an opportunity to start my own event planning company. I questioned myself: "Start a company? How? Doesn't it take a lot of money to start a company? What about office space?" I don't have any money. I've never done anything like this before. I could never be a boss! I don't know anything about event planning. NO WAY!"

The doubts came pouring into my mind. But, the opportunity sounded interesting and I thought it might even be fun. I wrote a business plan. Finally, I thought, writing all those marketing and business plans at USC was coming in handy. Looking over the plan, I saw that it made sense. I opened an event planning company called CLI Groups, Inc.

Where There is a Will, There is a Way

I started my company as a part-time gig. I started with just $100.00 in my bank and put the rest of the expenses on my credit card. I worked seven days a week. I paid my bills with the paycheck from my job and ran my new company on the side. I was determined to make it work. It was fun. Working hours upon hours, seven days a week made the time fly by. When I started making a little bit of money from my event planning company, it became even more fun! I was actually enjoying myself.

Six years later, I have several employees and I still LOVE what I do. I discovered all of this joy because I had finally made a decision that was based on what I wanted. I love what I do, and I make money doing something I enjoy.

I try to never let opportunities slip by or take them for granted. I have become a very strong entrepreneur. It's hard for me to remember a time when I was a young, shy girl, afraid to strike up a conversation; a girl who only made decisions based on what made other people happy.

New Opportunities Await

I recently had another opportunity come my way. Some of the people in my life say I must be crazy. They are sure I will quit and fail. What do you think goes through my head when I hear these things now? After all I've been through, I am finally at a point where I really don't care what they say. I did my homework, wrote a business plan, and determined that this new opportunity made sense. I like this new project and am ready to take it on.

Once you learn how to make decisions based on what's best for you and stop seeking the approval of others, you will come to know your true self. You can then take charge of your destiny. Growth comes from working through changes and making the tough decisions. I have finally come to trust my ability to make the right decisions to insure my future, and I wish the same for you. I hope you are inspired to make your own decisions based on your mind and your heart.

Spencer Horn is a leadership development expert at Rapport Leadership International - a leadership organization that directly impacts a company's productivity and growth by unleashing its employees' potential.

Businesses across the country look to Spencer for counsel and advice on developing productive, focused corporate cultures. He draws upon nearly twenty years of executive experience in performance-based leadership training, consulting, strategic planning, and public relations.

Spencer holds a bachelor's degree in political science and a master's degree in economics from the University of Utah. He has been married to his amazing wife, Jana, for over 24 years. Together they have five beautiful children.

Websites: *RapportLeadership.com*
Websites: *RapportConnection.com*
Twitter: *@spencerhorn*
Facebook: *spencer.horn*
Phone: *800-989-0715*

Chapter Thirteen

Who Can You Blame?

Spencer Horn

Most people don't want to admit they might be to blame when they make poor choices. It is easier to blame others or our circumstances when things don't go well. Conflict when neither side will admit responsibility nor blame is what makes lawyers rich!

"The Blame Game"

Often in our society, parents blame teachers for low test scores, teachers blame parents for unruly children, employees blame their bosses when work gets too hard, and citizens blame the government for their economic woes. There is an epidemic of "entitlement" mentality: thinking we deserve "the good life" without taking responsibility for earning such a life.

Winning starts when we take responsibility for who we are, where we are, and our actions. The choices we make and the behavior that we develop creates the results we desire. My life is filled with lessons that have taught me the power of personal responsibility.

Behavior That is Rewarded is Repeated

Experiencing the rewards of good choices will reinforce the behaviors that brought them. The consequences of bad choices will help you to learn from your mistakes. Be willing to accept responsibility for the results you achieve based upon your behavior and the choices you make.

Whose Fault is it?

I recently spoke with a friend who complained that he may lose his house. He was blaming the current president, who had promised economic relief to those that were in danger of foreclosure. He was stunned when I interrupted him to ask if the president or his government had signed his mortgage or if the bank had forced him to stop paying his mortgage. Of course not! HE had chosen to stop making the payments because the value of his home was less than the amount owed and he was struggling financially.

He argued that the banks had received government aid that was meant to help borrowers in his situation. He didn't want to accept the fact that when he chose to buy his house, **he assumed the risk** that the market value of his house may change. No one *forced* him to make that decision. When we have to deal with the consequences of our choices, we quickly learn to make better decisions. My friend's attitude and behavior were actually **preventing him from winning** because he was focused was on who to blame rather than on **finding a solution**.

Choose to Follow Role Models Who Have a History of Making Great Choices

My father was born during the great depression to a poor family in East Germany. During World War II, he was nearly killed for expressing his religious beliefs, which included defending people of Jewish descent. His life and the lives of his family were spared when he was conscripted into the Hitler Youth at the age of fourteen. He made a conscious choice that he would never kill anyone. As a result, he never did. Through many circumstances that can only be described as miracles, his life was spared. He eventually moved to Canada and then to the United States.

New Beginnings

There, he supported his family and paid for college by working as a janitor. One of the businesses he cleaned was a lithographic shop. He was interested in learning more so he offered to work for two weeks – for free – to demonstrate his ability in the hopes that the manager would then hire him. Before long, my father was not only working there, but he had become the manager of Warner Color Lab.

My father dropped out of college to work full time, and in a few years he decided to buy the business. He approached one of the owners, Mr. Warner, and said, "I have come to buy you out." Mr. Warner told him that he was not interested in selling.

My father then travelled to California to see the other owner, Mr. Fred Iverson. Fred was a wealthy man with interests in other businesses. When he asked "What is on your mind?" my father responded, "Fred, I have come to buy you out." Fred instead asked him to be his partner. My father responded by saying, "I would rather be the King of Monaco than the Prime Minister of France."

The next day, Fred put a stack of papers in front of my father and said, "You want to be King of Monaco. Here are the papers for you to sign." It turned out that Mr. Warner owed Fred money, so Fred was able to sell my father the entire business.

My father chose to take a risk and purchase the company using his own assets as leverage. He had no formal business education. Over a period of twenty years, he created one of the most successful color houses in the country. My father taught me about living your values. Regardless of your education, you can rise to success based on your commitment and desire. No one gave my father a handout. He won in business by taking responsibility for his results.

Choose to Accept Personal Responsibility

I learned about personal responsibility from my mother. In her late 30's, she was diagnosed with breast cancer. Ten years later, when I was just eighteen, she gathered me and my siblings to tell us she had been diagnosed with bone cancer and that the doctors had given her six months to live. She then very bravely announced that we were going to live life as if nothing had changed. She had chosen to make the most of the time she had with us.

She was an eighth grade English teacher, and she continued to teach despite her condition. At home, she would grade papers while resting on the couch. She loved teaching and she loved her students. They reciprocated her love and often came by the house to see her. My mother chose to live! She thought positive thoughts, sought the best medical advice, and even went to Mexico for experimental treatments because she believed they would help.

Precious Memories

Soon after, I was called to serve a mission for my church in Italy. Missionary service is an important part of our faith. It was challenging for me to leave, but my mother wanted me to serve. I left not knowing if I would ever see her alive on this earth again. After 14 months of service, I received a call that my mother was dying and I returned home immediately. The doctors did not think she would live until the weekend. She lived for six months more which gave us precious time together.

My mother chose to win. She never felt sorry for herself. She did not choose the cancer, but she chose how to deal with it. She fought bravely and spent quality time with her children. While I was away, she had written inspirational letters to me, never complaining about her condition. I am so grateful for her legacy of personal responsibility.

By contrast, my older sister has ignored our mother's legacy. She has chosen to live a miserable, unhappy life. She chooses to focus on the negative and is upset that her mother is not here to help her. She is a prisoner of her choices and fears; she lives her life as a victim, without joy or purpose. She has chosen to merely survive, instead of reaching out to win.

Be Coachable; Learn From Mistakes

Instead of feeling sorry for yourself, take feedback as an opportunity to grow. Upon graduating from college with my master's degree, I was hired as the general manager of an entertainment operation in Branson, Missouri. My boss was a friend and mentor. After a few months, he met with me and laid out the behavior he expected. Because I had been taught to take personal responsibility, I was not upset with my boss nor did I feel I was being treated unfairly. The choice was easy; I wanted to succeed so I made the necessary changes. Within six months I was promoted to Vice President of Operations. I was just twenty-seven years old.

Learning the Hard Way

I haven't always made great decisions, but I always accept responsibility and learn from my mistakes. At one point, I started a business without having done my due diligence or consulting my wife, who was against the idea. Four years later, we had depleted our savings and our home was in foreclosure. In the end, we were forced to give it back to the bank. This was devastating. I changed direction with my business, we found a nice rental house, and life continued. It was not the bank or the government that caused me to lose our home. It was a consequence of *my choices and actions*.

My friend who was losing his house thought my advice was harsh. I know first-hand how painful it is to lose a home. But blaming others for our predicaments only hurts us, and it gives away our power to change. If we believe our problems are generated **externally**, we may think we have no choices. If we think nothing we do will matter, we may choose to do nothing. When we **take personal responsibility**, we change our behavior and our outcome, creating an opportunity to learn, grow, and win. It all starts with our perspective and our choices.

Schall Adams is a wildly fun and transformational speaker who shares her love of life through teaching people to connect to their passions, express themselves, make a positive difference, and continue to grow and expand their capacity. Schall's unique "4 Keys" process helps people to "wake up and live!"

Schall speaks on expanding personal and professional capacity – including how to achieve optimal health, the importance of role models and mentoring, how to find the right mentors, and women's issues. She also performs with The Schall Adams Band.

She is the founder of **Girlfriend Mentors**, an international community that brings women together as mentors and role models. For more information, please visit Schall at:

> *Website: www.schalladams.com*
> *E-mail: info@schalladams.com*
> *Facebook: schalladams*
> *Twitter: @schalladams*
> *Phone: 775-412-1891*

Chapter Fourteen

It's an AMAZING Life!

Schall Adams

Many people just show up for life; they go to work, come home, eat dinner, have children and raise their families, but they **never truly connect** to who they wish to be in their life's journey. The truth is that our world is filled with wondrous possibilities, and that life itself is amazing. There is so much to experience and share. My journey is to help others create a life they WANT to live, deliberate and conscious of all the possibilities.

I was fortunate to have experienced an awakening to "my true self" – the real spirit inside of me. You, too, can enjoy such an experience. Many of us live our entire lives without ever discovering our true selves. Now, I am able to share how I created an incredible life and how you can use these same steps to create *your own amazing life!*

What is an AMAZING life? Here is how I define it. An amazing life is:

- A life that is connected to your true passions and vision.

- A life that expresses or monetizes your passions.

- A life of giving selflessly and making a positive contribution in the world.

- A life of *stretching yourself* and continuing to grow, expanding your capacity.

Get connected to your true passions

Getting in touch with your true purpose or passion is the foundation for an amazing life.

I have had the entrepreneurial "bug" ever since I was a teenager. After trying my hand at several different opportunities, I eventually discovered a passion for a healthy eating style called "raw foods." I took every class on the subject and became certified to teach it. I was off and running!

This quickly became the most successful business venture I had ever created. I was often featured on the news, was written up in several magazines, and I earned a 5-figure monthly income for the first time in my life. I was even asked to demonstrate and speak on a panel at the "Worlds Largest Raw Food Festival." Over time, though, the business began to deteriorate as I found myself becoming less and less passionate about the business of raw foods. I tried a lot of different ways to get it back on track.

Look for Clues

It's important to pay attention to yourself, your actions, and your thoughts as these will provide the keys to your true purpose. I realized that I was no longer reading books or watching videos about my industry. I wasn't learning or creating new information on raw foods anymore. Instead, I had gone back to reading books on motivation and on human potential, and I was attending seminars and trainings in person and online. I realized that I had spent most of my adult life reading books on human potential, motivation, inspiration, and personal development!

This is a clue for you! What do you spend your time thinking about, reading about, having conversations about, or researching? If you could be doing anything right now, what would that be? Don't try to qualify your answer. Suspend critical judgment. No matter what comes to your mind, do not downplay it by thinking, "I'm not good enough yet," "My spouse won't like it," or "I couldn't make money doing that."

My True Passion Revealed

I had been trying to get to a certain level in my business so that I could do what I really wanted to do, which is to **show people how amazing life is!** But, in my mind, I had created limitations around money. I believed that I had to be rich before I could teach in the field of human potential. I hadn't given myself credit for the knowledge and lifestyle I had already created. I hadn't honored the process of emerging from a dysfunctional childhood as a happy, productive adult.

So, when you do this exercise, look at yourself and your life as a whole. Again, keeping only that picture in mind, ask yourself: *"If I could do anything right now, what would that be?"* Once you answer, do you notice a difference in how you feel about yourself? Make a list of what you already know about your choice. Describe the experience of your growing awareness. This will help you to understand that you have something to share regarding the topic, and it will also help you to embrace new possibilities.

Express or monetize your passion

I hear many people say, "I don't know what I am passionate about," and what I find is that they really mean, "I don't know how I could make a living doing what I am really passionate about." Or, they have allowed life to conceal the things they really want to experience.

So, let's talk about how you will align your passions with your activities. Begin brainstorming on how you will express the passions you connected to in the exercise above. JUST START WRITING – write down every passion you think of and do not make judgments or dismiss anything that comes to mind. You could also brainstorm with a mastermind group in person or online.

Develop your authority and release your fear. Many people think they have to be a recognized expert before they can share something with the world. This is especially true when deciding to make a living at something. **The truth is, there will always be someone who doesn't know what you know.** If everyone waited to become a world-renowned expert before they did something, no one would do anything! It is through our *experience* that we become experts. Sharing what we know as we grow helps us to refine our expertise by using interaction with others as a guide. This is a proven process, and successful people know it. They get into action.

Make a positive contribution to the world

We often get stuck when it comes to promoting ourselves, but when you express what you love doing in a way that helps others, it is very easy to promote what you are doing. Make the connection between what you do and its effect on others, and you will reach heights of success that most people only wish and dream about.

Connect everything you do to others, especially your "life's work". How does your business help others? How do your hobbies help others? Be passionate about the relationships you create in this world and serve them wholeheartedly. Look at the whole of your life and ask yourself, *"How does my life impact others?"*

When you operate your organizations, your business, your activities, and your thoughts and emotions from a place of conscious engagement with others, it will empower you and others to reach higher and stretch further. Your view of the world will be broader, deeper, and more powerfully influential. Start today:

make a positive difference in the world with everything you say, think, and do.

Continue to grow and expand your capacity

We are responsible for our own lives. If you want more out of life, you must get more out of yourself.

When we feel like we may be failing, we often look for reasons to say, "It didn't work out." Many times we give up this way to save face and to avoid failing. We use a variety of sayings - "Wasn't meant to be" or "Everything happens for a reason" - but I believe that if we have really determined what our life's passion is and we are attempting to express it, then giving up is not an option. Instead, we need to look at expanding our capacity.

When I feel overwhelmed, outside my comfort zone, or beyond my capacity, that is when I consciously choose to expand. This is a moment of great importance. When you recognize what is happening, you can consciously choose to grow your capacity and manage the task at hand.

As I was developing "Girlfriend Mentors," there was a woman who I wanted to interview for the site. We were on the phone and she was criticizing my website. I had created it myself and it looked great in my browser with the settings I had used; her browser and settings were different.

I was so uncomfortable that I just wanted to get off the phone! Instead I hung in there and scheduled the appointment with her. After I hung up, I had to compose myself. It was in that moment that I truly understood the concept of *being outside your comfort zone.* This was a moment when I could grow or retreat. I chose to grow. Now, whenever I feel uncomfortable I simply take a deep breath and repeat one word to myself over and over: *"Capacity."* This changes my state of mind and makes me aware that this is a moment of growth for me.

If you take this to heart, you will experience something AMAZING happening within you. This is a tool that you can use to grow beyond your current capacity. If you find yourself saying, "It wasn't meant to be" or "Everything happens for a reason" – recognize that this is a moment of decision for you. Choose to grow or retreat. If you choose to grow, your life will be AMAZING.

Branded as "The Potentialist", Dion Jordan is recognized as a top authority on peak potential and personal development. An award-wining speaker, author, and consultant with more than twenty years experience, Dion has directly impacted the lives of thousands of people from several countries with his powerful and life changing speaking engagements, products, and live events.

He has been called on by Olympic gold medalists, professional and collegiate sports teams, corporate executives, ministers, and political leaders for his expertise in personal development and leadership. Dion is also the highly acclaimed author of several books, including his best selling, *"All That It Takes Is All That You've Got"* - a book dedicated to helping people live their dreams and reach their goals.

To have Dion Jordan speak and inspire your audience, please visit him at Dion Jordan Enterprises:

> *Website:* *www.DionJordan.com*
> *E-mail:* *LiveYourDream@DionJordan.com*
> *LinkedIn:* *DionJordan*
> *Phone:* *877-572-1704*

Chapter Fifteen

One Life to Live

Dion Jordan

Imagine that you are eighty years old, sitting on the front porch of your house, looking back over your life, reflecting about the things you have done and the things you wanted to do but never did. At that moment you realize that your life is almost at its end. Chances are you will be overwhelmed with one of two feelings.

One might be a feeling of total satisfaction. You lived the life you wanted to live and you did the things you wanted to do. Your life was not only successful in your own eyes, but it was meaningful. You have no fear of what tomorrow might bring because your yesterday and today brings you peace and fulfillment.

The other feeling might be dissatisfaction and regret. Why? Because you never did what you wanted to do with your life, and you know your time is almost up. You never fell in love or wrote that book; you never traveled like you wanted to or expressed your love to the ones who meant the most to you.

The worst feeling of all is realizing that your days are limited and that **you never really lived**. Regardless of what our religious beliefs might be, as far as we know we have just one life to live on this earth so we should make the most of it.

A True Story

When I was sixteen years old, I had a dream that changed my life forever. I dreamt that I had died. In this dream, I found myself sitting in the middle of a large auditorium with thousands of empty seats around me. It was pitch black. I was alone, scared, and could not believe my life was already over. Suddenly I heard a loud noise like a crash and a movie began to play. What I saw both amazed and terrified me. The movie was about me; the story of my life was being shown. I saw myself growing up as a child, crippled and unhappy. I had no friends, I had no smile.

The Dream Continued

I watched myself walking down the street kicking trash, all alone. This condition continued until I was old and alone, with a permanent look of depression and dissatisfaction chiseled in my face. As I watched this movie my eyes began to tear in disbelief and sadness.

Suddenly the movie was over. Immediately, on another screen, a second movie started. It was about me again. But this time it pictured me in a better, brighter light. I was so happy and full of life. People all around me were energized by my enthusiasm. As the movie went on, the better it got. I saw myself growing up, having a family, and living a life of both success and significance. This time as I watched, my eyes were not full of tears, but wide open – filled with pride and excitement. I looked around and I was no longer in an empty auditorium, but one that was filled with people completely engaged and inspired by my life on the screen. Then just as quickly as the movie started, it abruptly ended and the room once again went pitch black. I shouted NOOOOO!! And then I woke up. From that day forward, at age sixteen, I decided I was going to live my life as I saw it in the second movie...with no regrets...and fully appreciating and understanding that I have just one life to live!

A Life of No Regrets

How is the movie about your life going to play out? Are you going to live the life you dream of or are you just going to just dream of a better life? When you live a life following your true life passions, you bring something to this world nobody else can give; you bring your unique energy, delight, and service that radiates from the joy you find in living your dream.

If you decide not to follow your passion, something will be missing in the world that no one else can replace. After all, no one else can write your book but you; no one can start up a business like you. You are unique and no one can take your place. The great author Dr. Suess wrote, "Today you are you, and that is truer than true. There is no one alive who is youer than you!"

What do you want to stand for? What do you want out of this life? Below you will find ten simple but clarifying questions to help you discover your life's passion. Once you have answered the questions below, fill in the paragraph with the corresponding answers. You'll begin to see what is possible for your life!

10 Questions to Determine your Passion

1. What is your name?

2. What are you passionate about?

3. Before my life is over I will _____ - or die trying.

4. What special quality do you look for in a friend?

5. What do you love most about yourself?

6. What is your greatest gift to the world?

7. If you had one career-related wish, what would it be?

8. What is one thing you would do if you knew you couldn't fail?

9. What is your greatest fear that you feel has held you back in life?

10. Write your name once again.

My name is (1)_____ and I am passionate about (2)_____.

My life has meaning and my mission is clear. I am determined to (3)_____ and I will not be denied. When I walk into a room, people will know by my presence that I am somebody.

When it comes to others I will look for (4)_____ within them. When it comes to me, I will let the pride of my (5)_____ shine through.

I am valuable because of who I am and what I have to offer the world; I have a gift of (6)_____.

Today I have decided to live my dream of becoming a (7)_____, yet I reserve the right to change my mind. I have the tenacity and the audacity to (8)_____ if I so desire.

I will not shy away from my fear of (9)_____, but rather use all my fears as fuel to make me stronger and propel me wherever I want to go.

I am going to love the life I live and I will follow my heart because I know it knows the way. My name is (10)_____ and I am going to life the best life ever!

The Chicken and the Eagle

Have your heard the story about the chicken and the eagle? There once was an Eagle who laid its egg high on top of a mountain. On the bottom of the mountain there was a chicken coop full of chickens. Well one day when the eagle was out hunting for food, a strong wind came and knocked the eagle egg down the mountain all the way in the middle of the chicken coop. When the chickens saw this they were frightened. They all ran away except for one brave chicken who decided to sit on the egg.

After six weeks of sitting on this eagle egg, out popped a baby eagle. The baby eagle looked around and all it saw was chickens. The mother chicken, who had been sitting on the egg, looked down at the eagle and said, "You're a chicken. You're a funny looking chicken, but you are a chicken." So that baby eagle grew up believing it was a chicken. It ate chicken food, and went to a chicken school and got a chicken education; it grew up and got a chicken job.

It was living its life like a chicken until one day a real eagle flew by. When the real eagle flew by and saw this strange sight in the chicken coop, it decided to land inside and investigate. Once he landed all the chickens got scared and ran off. Finally the real eagle looked at the chicken-eagle and said, "Hey, what are you doing hanging around all these chickens?" The chicken eagle responded, "I am a chicken and I am just hanging around my brothers and sisters."

You were Meant to Fly like an Eagle

The real eagle responded, "You are not a chicken, you're an eagle! You should be flying and doing great things. Watch this." And the real eagle flew over the fence surrounding the chicken coop and started soaring in the sky. Meanwhile the chicken-eagle watched in amazement wishing it could do the same. When the real eagle finally landed, it looked at the chicken-eagle and told him, "You can do the same thing. The choice is yours, you can fly and be the great eagle you were meant to be or you can continue to live your life as a chicken." Then the real eagle flew away.

So what about you? Are you going to live your life like a chicken or an eagle? I hope you choose the latter. Remember you have just one life to live so let's make the most of it!

As a negotiations expert in the Hospitality industry, Darleen Ghirardi has saved her employers more than **one billion dollars** in the last fifteen years. In 2001, the hospitality industry was being challenged with major cost increases for all food and beverage products. Darleen created a cutting edge purchasing approach for controlling escalating costs and distributor's margins. Her new and innovative method has become an "industry standard" now practiced on a regular basis in the Las Vegas marketplace.

Darleen's life experiences and exemplary character have made her a sought after Certified Executive Coach who inspires others to achieve their goals and make good, self-empowering choices. You can contact Darleen at:

Website: *www.DarleenGhirardi.com*
E-mail: *Darleen@DarleenGhirardi.com*
LinkedIn: *darleenghirardi*
Twitter: *@dghirardi*
Phone: *702-281-7790*

Chapter Sixteen

The Right Path

Darleen Ghirardi

In 1995, I made a decision to change professions. After several years of working in restaurant management, I became interested in the field of purchasing. I was always a saver in my personal life, so the thought of being able to save money on a larger scale for a big corporation was intriguing to me.

A Step Down: Positioning Yourself for Future Greatness

A position as a Food & Beverage Purchasing Clerk became available at the hotel and casino where I worked, so I applied for the position and was delighted to make a successful transition. Many times, when we are driven by our passion, our friends tend to think we have lost our minds! It was not surprising to me that my friends thought I was crazy to go from a management position to that of a clerk. Rather than view this as a means to an end, they saw this as a demotion. I, on the other hand, considered it the **opportunity of a lifetime**...a true gift.

What I didn't know at the time was that my new boss, the food and beverage purchasing agent, had a friend in mind for the position; she was not excited that I got the job instead. Needless to say, I was not made to feel welcome. In fact, my boss did all she could to **make my life miserable** by creating ridiculous tasks for me to complete.

That Which Does Not Kill You...

One of my new boss's favorite tasks was to have me compile a complete list of what was purchased along with the item's brand name. Surprisingly, not all items are specified by their brand name so this created a good deal of extra work as there were hundreds of items. The only way I survived was with the help of the Receiving Department and their supervisor. Those employees wore freezer suits and would stand in the freezer and call out the brand names to me while I stood in the doorway. Otherwise, I would have had to stay in the freezer for twice as long.

After I rallied from this task, none the less for wear, my supervisor sent me to count potatoes. If the box read "80-count," I was to verify that there were indeed 80 potatoes in the box. I had to do this for every box.

That Which Does Not Kill You...

The saying, "That which does not kill you makes you stronger," is completely true. In spite of this pettiness, I loved my new job! I became a sponge, eager to learn everything I could from the chefs and the suppliers. In the purchasing profession, suppliers will embrace you with open arms once they determine that you are honest, ethical, and that you treat people fairly.

I'd been in my new position for about a year, when one of our supplier representatives approached me with a concern regarding my boss. One of our food manufacturers had a sports-themed promotion based on company purchases of their items. Our company had approved this promotion for key personnel in the Food and Beverage Department as well as the Purchasing Department. The promotion would offer awards such as leather sports jackets, baseballs, and other sports-related merchandise.

Sticky Fingers

The sales representative informed me that he was told by my boss to place all the award merchandise into the trunk of her personal vehicle. He did what she told him to, but felt compelled to tell me this when the executive chef kept asking him when he was going to get the leather sports jacket he had earned.

Although my boss and I did not always see eye to eye, it had never occurred to me that she might be capable of theft. I knew I needed to report what I had learned about the merchandise, so I told her boss, the Food and Beverage Director, and anxiously waited to see the outcome.

The Burden of Proof

Her boss requested that I obtain statements from the sales representative and call the manufacturer to obtain a list of the merchandise and its value. Once he had all of the backup documentation in place, he approached my boss, the purchasing agent. She denied it, and the director made the decision **to believe her**. That seemed to be the end of it.

Now, more than ever, I felt as though I was in an awkward and compromising situation, plus there was now another employee who was aware of the situation with my boss. I made the difficult decision to go to the Director of Human Resources, knowing that my career could very well be in jeopardy. In my life, it's always been easy for me to do the right thing. **Honesty and ethical behavior are part of my core values**.

This time around, more people were aware of the theft. The Director of HR involved the VP/General Manager of the property. Upon completion of the investigation, my boss was terminated. She never admitted taking the merchandise, despite the overwhelming evidence. And, she didn't go quietly; **she threatened my life**. I had to watch my back and be as vigilant as possible for a long while. I was given a security escort to my car after every shift.

Her boss, the Food and Beverage Director, lost a portion of his bonus as a result of his part in all of this. Meanwhile, I was in career limbo.

I took on the extra duties of my former boss while still keeping up with my own work, and waited to see who my new boss would be. There were several contenders for the job. I was also concerned that my boss's boss might let me go, since he was not happy with his diminished bonus, which was directly the result of his own actions regarding the theft.

A New Career: Over Before it Begins?

I was starting to believe my new career in Purchasing might be over. Imagine my amazement and joy when the company promoted ME to the Purchasing Agent position! They valued my loyalty to the company.

It wasn't until after my promotion that I discovered even more information about the situation with my boss. The company audited my department and, as it turned out, they appreciated and supported my decision to come forward more than I could have imagined.

As a result of my experience, I was determined to **succeed in my new career**. I did all I could to learn more about the industry and my work. In a short while, I was promoted to the Director of Purchasing position for two of the company's properties.

Within just seven years, the top purchasing job in the company became available. I expressed interest in the position and, thanks to the help of two mentors – one who taught me the ropes and one who helped me to believe in myself – I was promoted to Corporate Director of Purchasing. I had to prove myself, and it was not an easy ride, but it has been a fabulous experience.

Know Yourself

There are many times in life when it is challenging to stay focused and on-target. This is one reason why it's critically important to **surround yourself with positive people** ... those who build you up and believe in you. One of my mentors believed in me enough to give me my dream job.

There's nothing like achieving a goal you have set for yourself! I'll never doubt myself again, as I did when I first changed careers. Had I listened to others before taking that position as a clerk, I would have missed out on so many of the joys that have since come into my life. Sometimes, we just have to know in our hearts that we are doing the right thing and be prepared to accept the consequences. *We can never know how strong we are until our strength is tested.*

I can't imagine ever compromising my core values. Honesty, integrity, character, and honor are the cornerstones of your foundation and they show the world who you are and what you stand for.

Life is full of challenges; it is how we choose to deal with them that sets us apart from others and makes us who we are. I believe in setting the bar high; *it's that much sweeter when you reach it!* And, I've discovered that with each challenge I overcome and each goal I reach, my confidence grows. Yours will, too!

In today's world, many people are frightened when they find themselves in an awkward position. They keep to themselves, afraid of rocking the boat. For me, this was never an option. I believe we won't be able to move forward with our lives until we step up and **do the right thing**. It's not always easy to build a reputation for having a strong character, but for those of us who earn that distinction, it is the only path to take.

Ron Lee's career began on stage as a child actor. He later studied at the *National Institute of Dramatic Art*, where Cate Blanchett and Mel Gibson also trained and still has the same agent as Olivia Newton-John and Russell Crowe.

Experience in acting, stand-up comedy, and martial arts along with successful careers in direct selling and finance led him to perform at conventions that require a high-impact, interactive, memorable speaker to deliver the message.

Ron trains executives on four continents and helps people to dissolve psychological barriers using Eastern/Western philosophies, Universal Laws, Practical Metaphysics and Martial Arts. Ron regularly travels to the U.S. to speak and has a flat fee to cover expenses.

"The Corporate Ninja" helps to empower you to become what you need to be so you can do what you're destined to do.

> Website: *www.corporate-ninja.com*
> Email: *ron@corporate-ninja.com*
> Skype: *rlee01*

Chapter Seventeen

The Corporate Ninja - Revealed!

Ron Lee

Research has shown that our greatest perceived voids determine our greatest values in life. Whatever we think is missing in our lives becomes a priority. In the 1960's, a survey of America's self-made millionaires showed that 92% came from impoverished families that lived in towns of fewer than 10,000 people. What were their voids? Money and influence. Their priorities? Money and Influence.

What do voids and values have to do with my being a professional speaker? When I started school in the late 1950's in Australia, the country was in the midst of *The White Australia Policy*. This policy granted immigration officers a wide degree of discretion to prevent individuals from entering Australia. The Prime Minister, Edmund Barton, said, "The doctrine of the equality of man was never intended to apply to the equality of the Englishman and the Chinaman." Thus Australian cultural attitudes were established, and although the Act was officially abandoned in 1973, prejudice still exists amongst many members of society.

Being of Chinese ancestry, I was victimized, abused, and beaten up. I lost count of the derogatory, racist names that I was called. My parents and I were born in Australia, and I was just five when this started to happen so I couldn't understand why people were doing this. Our government called our country a "tolerant nation," yet they were unwilling to accept anyone who appeared to be different. Apart from that, my cultural heritage did not encourage self-expression.

So, what were my main voids? **PERSONAL POWER** and **SELF-EXPRESSION**. Consequently, my main values were also **PERSONAL POWER** and **SELF-EXPRESSION**. These were the two elements that my life was missing, and I wanted control over them more than anything.

In my early 20's, I couldn't tell a story or a joke to save my life, but my desire to claim my power and express myself was strong. I seized an opportunity to audition for training at the *National Institute of Dramatic Art,* the same acting school that trained *Judy Davis, Cate Blanchett,* and *Mel Gibson.*

Acting is fun but it's just pretending to be someone else. It does little for the self-expression void. However, some of the "method acting"techniques have been useful in adopting characters that I use in "hoax presentations" and they are great for spontaneity. In fact, I still have a very good agent who also represents Olivia Newton-John and Russell Crowe.

The Lesson? Everything you do contributes to your life purpose.

Over the next few years, I became a leading door-to-door salesman and later a financial planner. One night, in 1986, I sat watching a television talent show called *Star Search* with my girlfriend who dared me to go on and do stand-up comedy, so I did. Ah, the bravado that accompanies ignorance.

Three days after phoning the *Star Search* production office, I was auditioning with the five minutes of material that I had spent the entire weekend writing. Ten days after that, we recorded the show and I was to compete against the winner of the four previous shows. A stroke of fate had me as the winner.

The Lesson? If you don't know you can't do something, you will probably be able to do it.

One of the judges on that first show was Penny Heaton, the manager of *The Comedy Store*. Midweek, she phoned to ask if I would do a set at "The Store" on the following Friday and Saturday. Not ever having performed stand-up comedy before, I asked, "How long of a set do you want me to do?

"In the second spot, we only need you to do about twenty minutes. Can you cut your routine back to twenty?"

"Cut it back to twenty? Sure." I agreed quickly, though I wondered how I was going to pad my five minutes out to twenty!

Friday night came and the room was packed. The audience of 400 people included three bachelor parties of twenty to forty men each. I decided to work off them and managed to complete the full twenty minutes. Penny was impressed and invited me back to be the Emcee.

From there, I decided to work exclusively in the corporate arena. Soon afterwards, someone asked me, "What's the difference between a corporate humorist and a stand-up comedian?" "About sixty times the fee."

The Lesson? If asked to step out of your comfort zone, do it! The rewards will be far greater than your perceived risk of appearing foolish. Then, leverage your talent to influence the right people.

Seven years before my stand-up comedy debut on national television, I became interested in martial arts as a way to fill my personal power void, and was active in eight different forms including internal and external, hard and soft techniques. It would be a while before I was able to merge this knowledge with my passion.

After deciding to become a full-time professional speaker in the late 1980s, I handed over all of my financial planning clients to an associate. I sought out speaking advice from a master; in this case, a speaker marketing expert, the legendary Dottie Walters.

Dottie asked a lot of questions before suggesting that I should become a "Mutant Ninja Turtle". Dottie had the eccentricity that is a prerequisite for genius, and despite my explaining that they already existed and that they were cartoon characters, she kept insisting that I be a "Mutant Ninja Turtle".

Driving home from our meeting, I thought, "I just spent $300 to be told I need to be a cartoon character to succeed as a professional speaker. A Mutant Ninja Turtle! How am I going to market *that* to companies? It would be different if I was a corporate ninja. Hmmmmm ... Or perhaps *THE* Corporate Ninja! Eureka! That's it!" As I write this, Dottie is probably looking down now with that kindly, benevolent smile. This was how I came to brand myself as *"The Corporate Ninja."*

The Lesson? Find someone who knows what they are doing. Trust them, but also think it through.

I was once asked to speak at the National Speakers Association on *"How I Got Where I Am in the Speaking Business."* Before taking questions, I delivered just three bullet points:

1. What can you offer the clients? What benefits will they have after you leave?

2. Why would they book you over someone else? What is your uniqueness?

3. Open the phone book and make the calls.

All of the great philosophers whose works I've read agree that the meaning of life is to leverage our talents, experience, knowledge, and passion to serve as many other people as possible.

A year after I decided to burn my bridges and follow my passion, I earned 200% of my previous most successful annual income. Eighteen months after that, when I sought ways to add value to my clients' experience of *"The Corporate Ninja,"* expenses remained about the same while my revenue doubled again.

The Lesson? In all areas of life, especially in business, focus on serving and adding benefits to the lives of everyone we influence.

Today, I use a combination of Eastern-Western Philosophies, Universal Law, Practical Metaphysics, and Martial Arts to show you how to dissolve the psychological barriers that can keep you from your dreams. These techniques can also help people to enjoy improved health.

Many illnesses are psychosomatic. People have cured themselves of diseases diagnosed as "terminal." Roche, a pharmaceutical company, once engaged me to speak at a dinner and address 150 transplant surgeons on *"The Role of The Mind and the Spirit in The Process of Healing"* and *"Metaphysics in Relation to Science and Medicine."* Afterward, Professor Adrian Hibberd, a surgeon and lecturer in transplant surgery, gave a public endorsement of everything that I had said.

I also perform presentations as a fictitious character, Dr. Takashi Kinoshita, a successful Japanese industrialist who uses martial arts philosophies in management and group takeover strategies. For the past 21 years, it has been my signature presentation and is probably the main reason that 83% of my bookings are repeat and almost all of the others come from referrals.

The Lesson? In business and in life, be known for something specific and unique.

For every negative, there is a positive of equal magnitude. A business magazine recently surveyed forty successful entrepreneurs and all of them said that for every disaster there is an opportunity, and the bigger the disaster, the bigger the opportunity.

So, what was my "negative"... my "void"? **PERSONAL POWER** and **SELF-EXPRESSION**.

What is the positive side that has come from that? People in 360 client companies on four continents are empowering themselves to exceed their expectations in the seven areas of their lives, namely, *Career /Relationships, Family, Intellectual, Physical, Social, Spiritual,* and *Wealth.*

The Lesson? Know what your "negative" or your "void" is and discover how can you use it to serve others.

Karyne Morris is an entrepreneurial leader and executive coach. At twenty-two, she launched Academy Casting Team and Associates, a casting company in Los Angeles. Karyne soon shifted to selling assets. She launched KB Morris Real Estate, Inc., an **international corporate real estate** firm.

More recently, Karyne is applying her "natural, uncanny salesmanship skills" and her life skills to conquer Network Marketing. Karyne has been coaching individuals to help them achieve their lifelong dreams – whether on stage, in front of the camera, in a board room, or in a car. Her objective is to help people achieve their two most-desired goals: **personal and financial freedom.**

Website: *www.gunghotravel.biz*
Email: *kbmorris@lvcoxmail.com*
LinkedIn: *KaryneMorris*
Twitter: *@karynemorris*
Facebook: *karyne.morris*
Phone: *702-371-2223*

Chapter Eighteen

Standing at the Crossroads

Karyne Morris

We often find ourselves standing at a crossroads, wondering which path we should take. Regardless of your age or where you are in your life, there will always be opportunities to change direction ... to take a different path. You always have a choice.

Many people feel alone and worried when trying to choose the right path, hoping they'll succeed in selecting the one that will lead them to their "promised land" – where they can finally live the life of their dreams and enjoy great wealth, freedom, and security.

The truth is, life choices are simple. You just have to make a decision. And each decision you make will lead you to another and another. Nothing is forever, and there will always be new opportunities to make different choices.

My Crossroads

I stood at a crossroads ten years ago. I was in an accident that took the lives of two women. My world as I knew it was changed forever. My innocence had been taken from me. I suddenly found myself in a world of politics and rules that was foreign to me. I was completely lost.

Instead of looking around for new paths of growth and faith, I put my head down. I threw myself into my work – a woman out of control and out of touch with reality. Life went on around me, passing me by. The grass was growing but I was not. I was not dead, but I certainly wasn't living. I had chosen not to feel OR heal at this particular crossroads. I made my decisions based upon the most basic needs of survival. I wanted to make everyone believe that everything was okay, when it wasn't. I believed that if I could convince others, I might convince myself as well.

"Fake it till you make it" was my motto. In my real estate business, I created teams of great leaders. Together, we touched the lives of many people, amassed great wealth, and enjoyed the kind of professional success that most people only dream of. Yet I was never satisfied with my sense of self-worth. Professional success is no guarantee of personal happiness or satisfaction.

A Time of Even Greater Transition

Two years ago, I found myself facing another life-altering crossroads. This time, my body was broken and my instincts were dulled. The powerful woman who once lived inside me no longer had the energy to turn on the lights. I often considered giving up.

I remember looking at myself in the mirror and realized that I had touched many lives during my survival phase. I had created strong leaders. It hadn't been all bad. I started to understand and accept that I had a gift for motivating and leading them. I knew I could not waste such a gift. I couldn't continue living as I had been for so many years.

I had thrived as a successful real estate broker for more than sixteen years, I tried to move forward but, I found myself facing a complete lack of passion. What I was feeling at this point wasn't the typical frustration that brokers might feel when there is a shift in the economy and a downturn in the real estate market. Everyone was struggling. But for me, it was much more than that. My desire to succeed was gone.

When you've lived with something for so long and then it's suddenly not there, you really feel its absence. I no longer felt the sense of fulfillment that used to motivate me to move forward. I was literally stuck at a crossroads once again.

Two Simple Steps

The answer finally came to me. When you have achieved great success and everyone (including you) expects you to be "The Incredible Leader," *you lead!* I just didn't know exactly whom I would lead or where I would lead them. But at least I had realized that I needed to lead others. I looked for the right opportunity!

The first step to achieving success is to recognize an opportunity when it presents itself. The second step is to make a decision.

Step one: We are constantly being presented with opportunities. These opportunities require that we change. With change comes growth. I had been so alone, waiting for someone to give me the answers. The cure for becoming complacent, bored, or unmotivated is to try something different. I finally recognized an outstanding opportunity in a field that was new to me – networking marketing.

Step two: It was time to make a decision. I wanted to do something new, so I seized this opportunity and went from being a "Successful Queen Bee Real Estate Broker" to an aspiring expert in network marketing sales. Based upon my experience, it stood to reason that I would have similarly successful results, even though I was in a different game. But success was elusive, which was puzzling to me as I'd always been successful, regardless of my field.

Now, Step UP!

I had taken steps one and two: I had recognized an opportunity and I had made a decision. Network marketing seemed to me to be a new and exciting choice - and it was in sales, which was familiar.

I discovered that it wasn't enough just to make a decision. The power of the mind is amazing, but you must also step up to the plate. You must move forward once you have made your choice.

The key to making sure that a decision will work lies in the depth of your conviction. You must be one hundred percent on board. Once you have decided which path to take, take the RISK necessary to move full speed ahead with your goal firmly in mind!

Get the Help You Need

I wanted support for my new decision. While reaching out for help is typically a good decision, I made a critical error at this point. I allowed a friend to be my coach. I became so dependent upon her that our relationship became a weakness for me. Instead of growing my business, we played. I would set appointments with her, but they would get rescheduled. It was not a productive relationship in any way.

My friend had always known me as a powerful leader, so she assumed I already knew what I was doing with my new venture. Instead, I had gotten as far off track as one could get. Even though we may seek support, we still need to take full responsibility for our actions and our decisions.

Making new choices is a rebirthing process. Sometimes, when we make a choice outside of what we know, we feel FEAR; this is often said to be "False Evidence Appearing Real." Remember, though, that our new choices are not necessarily going to go over well with those around us – especially our families or our support team. This is why we need to have absolute conviction for our new passions. Don't let naysayers or dream stealers talk you out of our vision. It's important that you surround yourself with people who trust in you and who believe that you are capable of achieving your goals.

Author William H. Johnsen wrote, "If it is to be, it's up to me!" I understand exactly what he meant! So when my NEW coach told me that I had become a dependent leader, it took me less than a minute to pick myself up, embrace my independence, and make a decision to pursue my current path as a more independent leader.

Steps to Surviving Your Crossroads

When you find yourself facing a crossroads, make a decision. Simply choose the path that you believe will be the right one for you. Take ownership of your destiny ... if you don't, who will?

Know that in order for your choices to lead you to success, you will have to do the really hard work yourself. Even if you enlist the support of others, the bottom line is that your success is up to you. The job of your support team is merely to raise you up as you move forward.

The Gifts of Change

One unfavorable aspect of my work in real estate was the finite nature of the transactions I oversaw. I enjoyed coming in and helping new parties with a transaction, but once the sale closed, my job was done and my relationship with those parties would end. I had to constantly forge new relationships with strangers. My contact list grew, but building long-term, professional relationships wasn't feasible.

The unexpected gift I discovered in network marketing has been that I get to build long-lasting, productive relationships. I can now help others consistently – with no end in sight. As it turns out, this is what finally got me excited about work again. I am now in a position to give back and help others, offering them the solid leadership that comes naturally for me.

Leading teams allows me to give back. This is how I know I made the right choice by seizing this opportunity when it was offered. Through network marketing and public speaking, I am able to motivate more people and share my knowledge of – and appreciation for – life. I find it incredibly fulfilling to help my team members improve their lives.

Today, I seek out and build life partnerships, I embrace change as an opportunity for personal growth, and I treasure my time and my freedom. I am now able to dedicate more of my time to my family. And, it's not surprising that as I've stepped up to my new challenges, I'm also starting to achieve greater financial freedom... all on my terms.

If you are standing at a crossroads right now, ask yourself if you are committed to change? If the answer is "yes" then take just one step today. Make it simple, make your decision, and make it work for you.

Les Brown is the leading authority on releasing human potential and enhancing lives. A renowned professional speaker, personal development coach, author, and television personality, Les has risen to international prominence by capturing audiences with electrifying speeches - challenging audiences to live up to their greatness. You can watch Les in action in "Beyond the Secret" and "The Compass."

Les is the recipient of the National Speakers Association's highest honor and has been selected as one of the **World's Top Five Speakers** by Toastmasters International. Les trains others to become better communicators and speakers as well, and currently works with more than 3500 clients. His network enables all people to learn how to inspire others to new levels of achievement.

Les Brown is a master speaker who continues to reinvent himself to positively change the world. Visit Les at:

Website: www.LesBrown.com
Phone: 800-733-4226

Chapter Nineteen

Kill a Mosquito with an Ax to Conquer Your Goals

Les Brown

Many people often question my drive, intensity, and persistence when I am reaching a new goal. Perhaps you would consider me over the top too. Why? Because I don't stop until I get it!

When I am focused on a goal, that's all I see. Often in life, people will set a goal. But then they see all of the obstacles and challenges standing in the way and decide not to pursue it.

Instead of giving cute anecdotes and encouraging mottos for reaching your goals, I will simply tell you this: when pursuing something new, take no prisoners! In fact, *"Kill a Mosquito with an Ax!"*

Chopping Down a Tree

Imagine the physical force it takes to cut down a tree. Hitting the firm bark, chip by chip, piece by piece, and finally, after hours of sweating, with achy muscles and blistered hands, you see only a small dent in your efforts. In spite of extreme fatigue, you know that if you continue to hit the exact same spot for another two to three hours, you will succeed at chopping down the tree.

Now close your eyes and visualize a person doing this work with a steak knife; it seems foolish doesn't it? Perhaps the person really doesn't want the tree to fall, or they intend on hitting the tree with a steak knife for the rest of their life. We know they surely won't see results any time soon!

Do You REALLY Want to Reach Your Goals?

I use this illustration to bring to life how casual some people are when they are looking to accomplish their goals. Have you ever heard someone say, "I have to stop over-eating" while they are stuffing their mouth with food? Or maybe you've heard someone say "I'm saving my money to start my business," when in fact they have just purchased their second state-of-the-art flat screen television! We all know people like that; in fact I used to be one of them.

I thought conquering my goals meant writing them down, looking at the goals every day, meditating on them, and imagining the goal in my head, and that by one miraculous way or another, I would achieve that goal without any hard work or personal sacrifice. And if that didn't work, then I would tell my goals to other people and hope they would make those goals come to pass. As we know all too well, this thought process is crazy!

Use Extreme Force

So, why I do I say *"Kill a Mosquito with an Ax"*? I'm glad you asked! Picture someone tenderizing a steak with a jack hammer or toasting a marshmallow with a blow-torch. It may seem bizarre, but using passion, hard work, and extreme force to achieve your goals is what makes most people successful.

Here are a few reasons why these work.

It lets your friends and associates know how serious you really are.

People Can Make You Sick

I love friends and the value of good relationships, but there are some relationships I have to keep at a distance. I firmly believe you have to move outside of your normal relationships to really make something happen in your life. Why?

Living in the Past

Well…some people know too much about you and will not let you forget it. I still have some childhood friends who recall how bad I was in school or how many times I screwed up early in my career. When pursuing your goals, you don't need anyone reminding you of how messed up you *used to be!*

That's why you **"kill a mosquito with an ax"**; because it's crazy! If people say "You're crazy," look them square in the eye and tell them, "I know." Doing the same thing the same way and expecting a different outcome is even crazier!

It moves naysayers, obstacles, and unnecessary people out of the way. (They may get hurt in the process.)

Move...Get Out of the Way!!!

Have you ever had to knock down a piñata, blind-folded in a crowded room? Sure, it's a fun game, but when the game player has a bat in his hand, dangerously swinging back and forth trying to connect with the candy-filled, hanging toy, people move themselves and belongings out of the way to avoid being in the line of fire and getting hit!

Hit it Hard!

To reach your goals, you have to hit hard because doubt will come, financial issues will linger, family concerns will arise, and other events that could throw you off course will happen. Going hard keeps you focused and ignorant of skepticism. It boosts your intensity and drive for meeting future goals.

If I Did it Before, I'll Do it Again

It feels good to accomplish your goal. In fact, when you reflect on the process, you'll say, "It wasn't that bad after all." Before you know it, you'll start to feel fearless and daring, (not reckless and risky), and completely unafraid to take on new challenges and reach new heights.

Reaching your goals does not mean you defy everyone's advice or opinion. It means you have to listen with a different ear. Don't take everything into consideration, because some people are wrong. However, do listen for feedback. Be aware and accepting if someone else has another strategy for you that makes sense and could make your process easier.

I've enjoyed my journey and I still have fun climbing new mountains. And, in case you see me walking down the street with an ax in my hand, move out of the way! I'll be on my way to my next goal...a new challenge!

Christine Ferguson is an award-winning expert with more than fifteen years of experience in marketing, sales, and public relations. Christine speaks on leadership, marketing, innovation, and personal development.

Christine delivers authentic, compelling messages that inspire others to action.

She has been an entrepreneur, manager, director, and leadership team member for companies of all sizes – from small businesses to Fortune 500 companies.

Christine is both an Ambassador of Leadership and Master Graduate of Rapport Leadership International, a former Certified Professional Résumé Writer, as well as a New York University and University of Phoenix alumni.

To contact Christine, please visit:

Website: *www.christinenferguson.com*
E-mail: *christine@christinenferguson.com*
LinkedIn: *christinenferguson*
Twitter: *@chrisnferguson*
Phone: *702-278-9732*

Chapter Twenty

Your Dream Won't Find You

Christine Ferguson

"Maybe one day something good will happen in my life to give me hope and inspiration," said my relative Julia. "Huh?" I replied. "You mean you're simply *waiting* for some good fortune to fall into your lap?"

Julia and I had been on the phone for over an hour, and she'd been going on about how she'd lost hope for the dreams she once had. "I've given up on my dream because I'm too old for that career and there isn't anything else I'm passionate about," she said. This conversation was not new. I'd heard those words from Julia before. No matter what recommendations I made, she had the **EXACT** reasons for why it wouldn't work.

I recommended the book **"Second Acts"** – which is filled with real-life success stories of people who thought they were too old, too young, or too *whatever* to achieve their dreams. I also recommended the Heath brothers' book **"Switch,"** which is about how to implement change when change is hard.

Julia's excuse was that she is not a reader. "Well, how about an audio book?" I suggested. "You don't get it," she said. "I have no follow through. I will never follow the books' recommendations." **The excuses went on and on;** everything from "I have emotional issues" to "there is no hope for me."

Perhaps Julia does have "emotional issues," and she may need help beyond what I can provide. Yet she does little to find solutions and, naturally, she even has excuses for why she doesn't seek help: "I have no desire." "I give up." "This is my destiny." The problem with Julia is that she sees obstacles instead of opportunities. She makes excuses instead of taking action. She waits for help instead of seeking it.

I Want to Live!

The people who have appeared in the television series *"I Shouldn't Be Alive"* fascinate me. Each episode includes dramatic reenactments of individuals who have endured incredible ordeals over a period of several days. These stories of human survival and the will to live run the gamut - from being lost in the ocean to being stranded in some remote, snowy wilderness. One evening, I watched an episode about a group of boys that were lost in the Grand Canyon.

After several days, their bodies began to succumb to the extreme heat and the lack of food and water. Like many of the others from previous episodes, they began thinking they may not make it out of their situation alive. One of the boys fell asleep and dreamt his family was attending his funeral. It was then that he woke up, **determined to live!** After convincing his friends to take a death-defying climb down the face of a mountain to get water, the boys found help. Unbelievably, they stumbled upon a group of doctors who had been kayaking. One minute later, and they may not have been rescued.

That's when I was hit with the analogy between people who seek help to save their lives and people like Julia who make excuses and wait for help in order to achieve their dreams. It is no secret. When you want to achieve a dream, it is not going to come looking for you. *You have to go and find it!*

Those people who were lost in the ocean, the desert, or the jungle realized that no one was going to find them. They had to find help. They made the critical decision to do something frightening: swim out into the ocean or climb over a mountain to seek help. There was no time for excuses. They got out of their comfort zones and took that first step toward what looked like an impossible task.

The Secret is ... There is No Secret

There is no great secret to anything I am about to share with you. In fact, some of the most successful people in the world have used these techniques to attain their dreams:

Your Mind is a Powerful Instrument; Use It!

"Your dreams are all possible because of three pounds of gray matter," were the words famed

159

neurosurgeon Ben Carson heard during his residency at Johns Hopkins University. Successful entrepreneurs like Russell Simmons are examples of this philosophy. A few years ago, Simmons was a guest on **"The Oprah Winfrey Show."** During a Q & A session, an audience member asked his advice on starting a successful business. *"Everything you need is up here,"* said Simmons, pointing to his brain.

Whether your dream involves becoming wealthy or spending more time with your loved ones, begin to achieve it by turning down the negative thoughts in your head - the voices that say you won't achieve your dream because _____ (fill in the blank). An example might be, *"I won't achieve my dream of being successful because I don't have a college education."*

When a negative thought pops into your head replace it with a positive one, such as why you are grateful for something in your life. Focus on the gifts you DO have. Say something like, *"I WILL achieve my dream of being successful because I am smart."* Believe me, this takes both practice and patience. If you start by changing the way you think, you will be taking a step in the right direction by allowing your "three pounds of gray matter" to work for you.

Be Like Albert Einstein

In the History Channel biography, **"Einstein,"** it is reported that Albert Einstein would sit and ponder a problem for **hours, months or even years.** You may be surprised to learn that

Einstein believed he would be a failure in life. We all know how that turned out, despite the fact that he experienced fifteen years of setbacks in proving his **Theory of Relativity**. "Using only his mind and a pencil, Einstein made bizarre discoveries," said one of the History Channel interviewees. Become like Einstein; spend some time sitting, thinking, and taking notes about going after your dream. It will be well worth it!

Swim, Hike, or Climb for Help

Like the survivors of **"I Shouldn't Be Alive"** who swam, hiked, or climbed their way out of a terrifying situation to get help, you too must **seek the help of others** to get you on the road to success. If someone doesn't know you are drowning in despair, they won't know to throw you a lifeline.

In 2008, my financial health was poor. I was offered a job in Las Vegas, which would mean relocating from Georgia where I had been staying temporarily with my sister. My plan for relocating and moving in with a friend who lived in Las Vegas fell apart. I was devastated. Suddenly, I had to scramble to find my own place. As much as I hated to ask, I got help from my family. Within just one year, I was back on my feet. I was not only able to repay my loan, I also bought my first house!

Let Go of Your Ego

Some people have trouble letting go of their ego when it comes to asking for help. They are afraid of what others may think of them.

They continue to suffer while waiting for some miracle to save them. By letting go of your ego and opening yourself up to asking for help, you will *put yourself in a position to receive all that others are willing to give.* Others may form judgments or opinions about you; some people just do that. You get to rise above that! You cannot afford to let what others think of you prevent you from getting closer to your dream.

Tap an Accountability Partner on the Shoulder

Like Julia, you may get "fired up" about a dream and then later find you've lost your enthusiasm. She will often say to me, "I am just not like you." It's good to partner with someone who is different from you, who will support your dreams by bringing their own gifts into the mix. Remember to **see opportunities... not obstacles**. Find one or more people whom you know will be there for you, and arrange for them to check on your progress regularly.

If you want to get ahead in your career, for example, find someone who is willing to provide you with guidance and follow-through. **This is what mentors do.** If you don't know anyone, ask friends and associates if they know someone in your field who might be willing to help. Mentors enjoy helping others to reach their dreams. The Internet is also a terrific resource for finding people and groups that will support you.

On the road to success, you may experience a bumpy ride, make u-turns or get off at the wrong exit. This is not unusual. Success comes with its share of challenges. **PUSH ON!** You will soon learn to see these moments as opportunities. The challenges make your accomplishments even sweeter. And when you finally get to where you are going, you will be in a position to *share your experience* with others just as I've shared my experience with you. Your dream won't find you, so go find it!

Charles Clawson possesses a unique combination of experience as an attorney and a CPA, combined with a gift for social skills, which all come together to make him a tremendously successful entrepreneur.

Charles left a traditional law firm to create and manage Commonwealth Title. Three years later, he founded Noble Title. Since opening in May 2007, Noble Title has grown to be the 8th largest title company in Nevada.

Charles is actively involved in his church and his community. He enjoys running, exotic cars, and helping other people. Happily married with five children, Charles says that the day he met his wife was the best day of his life.

Please visit Charles at:

Website: *www.NobleTitle.us*
E-mail: *cclawson@nobletitle.us*
Phone: *702-212-5500*

Chapter Twenty-One

By Small & Simple Things

Charles Clawson

My toes are in the sand of Huntington Beach as I write this. I'm here with my most important employees on a weekend retreat with our families. Although we're at this gorgeous beach now, the story of how I launched a title & escrow company during one of the most challenging housing markets in history – "The Great Recession" – oddly begins at a BMW dealership many months ago.

I founded my company, **Noble Title**, shortly before the economic crash that occurred in the fall of 2007. I designed Noble Title to be the **"Ritz Carlton of title companies."** That is who we are; that is what we do. I am, in fact, a *"Connoisseur of Customer Service,"* because I know how people want to be treated. When I see employees helping others in considerate, thoughtful ways, I know that is how I want to treat my clients.

I once heard a Ritz Carton employee say that "anyone can build a beautiful hotel, but the thing that makes a Ritz Carlton different is *the people that it puts inside the building."* This idea is consistently supported by successful businesses that understand the importance of having the best people working for them. I whole-heartedly endorse that counsel. But, as a leader, what do you do once you've got the right people inside the building?

Discovering the secrets

When I started my title company, I wanted the quality of our customer service to be its most important, distinguishing characteristic. I wondered how I could train my staff to deliver such exceptional service. After all, **what defines outstanding customer service to one person may not be that special to another.** It is subjective and based upon our diverse upbringings, opportunities, and experiences.

I determined the best way for me to train my staff about customer service was to take them to other businesses so that we could all be on the same page. We began to visit other companies, **"secret shopper-style,"** and afterward we would discuss the positive and negative aspects of our experience.

A telling test drive

I love cars, and the more exotic, European, and expensive the car, the better. I decided to take some of my staff members to test drive the **"Ultimate Driving Machine."** Upon entering the BMW dealership, the receptionist failed to greet us. Instead we initiated the conversation by requesting a test drive of an M5.

Without even acknowledging the request, she lifted the telephone and paged a salesman to the front desk. She finally looked at me and said, *"Someone will be here in a minute."* We stood around at the receptionist's desk for a while. We noticed some chairs and went over to sit down and wait.

The salesman came and gave us a great test drive in a **"wickedly sweet M5."** We talked about BMW, exchanged contact information, and said our good byes. As we walked past the receptionist's desk, she said ... nothing.

A better experience

Back in the office, we debriefed the experience. We noted several minor issues that could have made a tremendous difference. First, the receptionist could have greeted us with a charming, faux-German, *"Hallo, velkome to BMW. Vould you like to take a test drive in the ultimate driving machine?"* That would have 1) immediately set the tone for a *German* car company and 2) sent the message that the company *wanted* me to take a test drive (a very important step in closing a car sale) and 3) *it would have made the experience a lot more fun.*

Next, the receptionist could have identified our salesman: *"Karl will be here shortly to take you on your test drive. Is there a particular model and color you are looking for?"* Then, she could have invited us to have a seat while we waited. As Karl arrived, the receptionist could have said, *"Hallo Karl, this is Charles. He'd like to test drive a black M5."* Imagine the impression that the dealership could have made on me up to that point.

Finally, as we were leaving, the receptionist could have said, "Auf Wiedersehen, Charles. *Please come again soon.*" Wow! I get excited just thinking about owning a BMW dealership and providing that kind of **über experience** for my customers. **Can you imagine how cool such an experience would be for YOUR customers?!**

Ask yourself: *"What would it have cost that BMW dealership to have created the extraordinary experience?"* Answer: $0. The experience I described requires only 1) a manager (leader!) with a vision and 2) a receptionist with a personality and the ability to speak with a German accent.

I'm not telling BMW how to run its business; I'm telling you how *I think BMW could have created an incredible experience* for it's customers – an atmosphere that would have been different, exciting, and fun, and one that would have made me want to come back for more. Businesses can generate ALL of those emotions in a customer at *no extra expense;* outstanding customer service doesn't cost a dime! But it CAN affect a company's bottom line. It only requires someone who cares and who really understands what is happening to make a difference. This is a perfect example of how *"by small and simple things are great things brought to pass."*

We continue to "secret shop" other businesses. The staff at Noble Title has been trained to *look for opportunities* to provide their clients with extraordinary service. We continue to "cherry-pick" from the best experiences and incorporate those ideas into our own impressive customer service. The culmination of those practices **enables us to treat our clients like royalty.** The royal treatment includes greeting clients by name, offering a menu of complimentary beverages and snacks, and making sure that we have fresh-cut flowers in every conference room.

Service Fit for a King...or a Queen!

Providing **world class, over-the-top service** is what has enabled Noble Title to thrive in the midst of "The Great Recession." I've told my staff that no matter how bad the economy is, there will always be business for those who deliver their best. As my staff focuses on serving our clients, I focus on my staff. **If I expect my staff to treat my clients like royalty, then I must treat my staff like royalty.**

Every summer, Noble Title treats its escrow officers, title officers, and sales reps to a fun retreat. These are some of my most important staff members. Last year, we took a cruise to Mexico. This year, we took everyone to Huntington Beach. As always, the employees were invited to bring their spouses. The more the merrier! **We maximized the fun and minimized the meetings.** After a long jog on the beach, we all met for a buffet brunch. On Saturday night, we enjoyed a bonfire on the beach. S'mores taste better with good friends, a little sand, and some salt air.

The primary feeling that I have for my employees is **gratitude.** I appreciate the hard work they do on behalf of our clients. I'm thankful for their loyalty and dedication. I recognize their efforts to maintain and exceed our company's high expectations.

Every day, the selfless sacrifices they make on behalf of the company's clients help reinforce our reputation for extraordinary customer service. Because they mean so much to me, I enjoy doing little things to make their jobs more fun and exciting.

Fun and Games

We foster an environment of working hard and playing hard. Some of our more recent shenanigans include playing bingo at the office. That may not sound extraordinary, but we play it over the paging feature on our telephone system. We make sure we are not disturbing any clients in the conference rooms. Winners receive movie tickets, gift certificates, and other prizes. We have company contests via email. Once I asked who could tell me the winner of the 1985 Eurovision Song Contest. The answer was Bobby Socks from Norway. There was a prize for that, too.

Some games have been more memorable than others. Once, we played a version of the old television show, ***"Fear Factor."*** I purchased a blender and I put a happy meal from McDonald's in it – a hamburger, French fries, and an orange soda. When lightly blended, a happy meal makes a stinky, chunky drink. Contestants had to drink a full Dixie cup, swallow and keep it down for 30 seconds. A runner-up got to take the new blender home and the winners received over-night stays at local Las Vegas resorts.

The bottom line

These prizes cost money, but my employees are worth it. Relative to our financial strength, these gifts are small and immaterial. But these little things make a big difference to my staff. *The games and prizes are FUN.* Do you go out of your way to make sure that the people in your office get to have fun? These games keep my staff positive and optimistic ... another example of how greatness can come from small and simple things.

I hope that through these stories, you will be inspired by my commitment to my clients and my staff and think of ways you, too, can develop a similar environment at your business. The better I treat my staff, the better they treat my clients. It is that simple. For Noble Title to thrive in an economy that was crushing start-ups every day, I knew that we needed to really deliver on all fronts. In my life, I have experienced tremendous results from that concept. You, too, can experience the same success. Ultimately, it comes from the idea of treating others as you would want to be treated. That in turn reinforces our company motto: *all for one and one for all.* Best wishes from your friend in Las Vegas, "The Connoisseur of Customer Service."

Nationally recognized health and fitness expert Chris Freytag has been motivating, coaching, and inspiring audiences everywhere for more than twenty years. Her passion for fitness and nutrition backed by her degree in journalism and communication makes her a popular speaker at corporate meetings and wellness events. Audiences leave with practical takeaways to achieve greater overall health.

Chris is a contributing editor to **Prevention Magazine**, and is a regular guest on **QVC** and the **NBC** affiliate in Minneapolis. She is on the Board of Directors for the American Council on Exercise. Chris has authored three books, two cookbooks, and regularly produces fitness DVD's.

Chris is the founder of Motivating Bodies, Inc., a provider of personal training, corporate training, and online products and services.

> *Website:*   *www.chrisfreytag.com*
> *Linkedin:*   *chrisfreytag*
> *Facebook:*   *chrisfreytag1*
> *Twitter:*   *@chrisfreytag*

Chapter Twenty-Two

Three Simple Steps to Improve Performance

Chris Freytag

The finish line is just the beginning of a whole new race. -Unknown

My oldest son was just eight years old when he stood with my husband, watching me run my first marathon. I was joined by thousands of participants. As we passed my son he exclaimed with concern, "Dad ... Mom's never going to win this race!"

I still laugh when I think about his innocent but misguided belief that I was actually running the marathon to win it. My goal was merely to finish the race, no matter how long it took me. Finishing the marathon felt great ... and it gave me the opportunity to explain to my son that the event wasn't about winning, but rather it was a milestone in my life.

As a high school student in the early 80's, I had a passion for exercise. I loved running and the feel of the endorphin rush. In college I was still a cardio addict, partly driven by calorie burn, but mostly driven by the mental clarity cardio delivers. I had a running partner and we'd run, gossip, and sweat. Realizing that fitness had no clear cut career path back then, I decided to major in my other passion which is journalism ... talking, sharing and writing about events and issues. Fast-forward twenty-plus years and I find myself lucky enough to have combined my passion for both fitness and journalism into a dream career.

I am an author, a fitness trainer, and a motivator, and I am passionate about helping others to lead healthy lifestyles. Over the last twenty years, I have helped thousands of people lose weight and get fit. Thousands more watch me on television giving tips and exercise options, and have downloaded my exercise videos and used my DVD's. But I am also the mother of three teenagers, a wife, a neighbor, a sister, and a friend. And, like you, I am trying to lead a healthy and fulfilling life in the midst of a crazy, busy world.

Good Health Equals Better Performance

My goal is to inspire my audiences to take ACTION towards achieving better health. There is a vital link between good health and great performance. Whether on the job, on the athletic field, or in everyday life, healthy people have more energy and are said to be 40% more productive than unhealthy people.

Good health is multifaceted; it a combination of three factors: 1) Your physical being, 2) Your diet, and 3) your emotional state. When these parts work together, they create a very powerful sum.

A journey towards getting fit and healthy begins by looking within. I have always said, "Genetics loads your gun but environment pulls your trigger." Researchers report that while genes play a part in your health, **you have a large percentage of personal control** when it comes to defining your attitude and how you take care of yourself. Isn't it interesting that the hardest thing for us to change is *ourselves?*

Quick Dramatic Results

In my years as a personal trainer, I've witnessed a phenomenon: every January, fitness clubs across the nation fill with well-intentioned people who have big plans for physical transformation. By the end of February, almost all of those newcomers are gone. When people don't see quick, visible, dramatic results, they tend to get discouraged and quit.

According to research, the reality is that it takes approximately 60 days to form a human habit.   So the key to success is making small and doable lifestyle changes that you can sustain, and then adding on to those changes each week.

Physical Being: Move Your Body

I love morning exercise, and for me, a workout at 5:30 am is the yin to my yang. I grab a quick cup of coffee and a banana as I head out the door to the gym, and get it done before I start the work day. But when I find a client that absolutely won't go for morning workouts, then I suggest another time of day that works. You see, what you may find is that what works for you is a little different than what you read or heard on TV. You may just have to bend the rules every so often to fit in a workout so you will actually do something rather than nothing.

Any movement is good movement. Dance, run, walk, swim - do what you like to do and do it often. Whether you have 10 minutes or 60, get active. Rather than hang yourself on the excuse of "lack of time," make the most of your exercise minutes. Intensity is the key to exercise and it trumps time in most instances. A common complaint I hear is, "I walk 5 miles a day but I don't see any results." My reply back is this: "What is your intensity?"

Pick up your pace, and your twenty minute workout can yield better fat melting results than your half-hearted sixty minute walk. You use two types of fuel when you exercise: fat and glucose. (Carbohydrates/sugars break down into glucose in your body.) Your body uses more fat as its fuel choice when walking at a moderate pace.

However, your calorie burn is also moderate. When you pick up the pace and walk or run with high intensity, your body uses more glucose as fuel but burns calories at a faster rate. Science proves time and again that the reality is still **"calories in vs. calories out"** regardless of the fuel used when trying to lose significant weight. Therefore, doing something is better than nothing, so while you're at it, ***work hard!***

Eating Healthy: Your Diet

You are what you eat...literally! We've all heard or said, "I cheated and had a piece of cake." Unfortunately, there is a fundamental problem with this line of thinking that works against each and every one of us.

It's about choice not cheating. If you allow yourself to attach negative values to certain foods and negative messages to yourself for eating them, you are setting yourself up for failure. And, when we *think* we have failed, we feel guilty and are more likely to give up.

Avoid the trap of an unforgiving all-or-nothing attitude or reasoning like "I blew my food plan with one cookie so I might as well have six!" Choosing to eat one cookie isn't blowing it; I couldn't live without a good cookie every so often!

Clean Eating

I have been talking about "clean eating" for the last two decades. My definition of clean eating is choosing foods that come from plants, animals, or trees - foods that are as close to their natural state as possible, such as fresh fruits and vegetables, legumes, whole grains, low fat dairy, lean meats, poultry and fish. In addition, much of clean eating is about preparation; it's not always what you eat as much as how it's prepared. For example, chicken is one of the healthiest protein sources when grilled or broiled, but when deep fried, it's a very poor choice.

Challenge yourself to clean up your eating. I've found that I can make dinner for three hungry teenagers in less time than waiting in line at the drive thru during rush hour. Along the same line, I advise my clients to rearrange the letters in "DIET" to spell "EDIT". Edit your food choices and pay attention to both the quality of your food and the amount you choose to eat. Try **moderation** rather than **deprivation**. It's not rocket science...it's about choices.

Attitude: Your Emotional Well-Being

Staying positive and optimistic will help too. My kids will tell you that ever since they were toddlers, the daily question in our house was, "Is the glass half empty or half full?" Your attitude will ultimately determine your success. We all have obstacles in our way but a "can do" attitude beats mere talent any day of the week.

When told, ***"Eat healthier and get more exercise,"*** most people hear, ***"Deprive yourself and sweat to death!"*** THAT is where the mental block comes in. This is why the third component to healthy living is having the right attitude; it will give you the chance to get that mental edge.

Aristotle said, "We are what we repeatedly do." A mental edge isn't something you can acquire before you get started. It's something that grows inside you and gets a little bit stronger with every healthy decision you make.

Achieving Improved Performance

So the bottom line is move more, eat healthy, and you will perform better in all aspects of your life. Make little adjustments and changes towards healthier living. With repetition and determination, it will sink in.

Abe Lincoln put it beautifully when he said, "Most folks are about as happy as they make up their minds to be!" I'm living my dream thanks to these three steps. See where new steps can take you.

Zach Johnson is a highly sought-after Internet and social media marketing authority. He has worked with some of today's best selling authors, including Tony Robbins, Jorge Cruise, and T. Harv Eker.

Zach's company, ZBiz, Inc. generates massive results for its clients, and does so at hyper-growth speeds. Through the ZBiz Internet marketing strategy, Zach is able to recruit Facebook "likes" – which translate brilliantly to revenue. With his help, a start-up can easily experience a $200,000.00 spike in revenue in their first 90 days.

ZBiz, Inc. is a full-service marketing agency that is on a mission to guide and direct companies into the future of marketing. Their unique proprietary approach delivers quality customers at a pace that is unrivaled by traditional sales and marketing methods.

Facebook: *ZachJohnson*
Facebook: *ZBizInc*
LinkedIn: *ZBizInc*
Twitter: *@ZBizInc*
E-mail: *Zach@ZbizInc.com*
Phone: *858-866-9451*

Chapter Twenty-Three

The ZBiz Marketing Manifesto: Your Key to Unlocking Internet Dollars

Zach Johnson

What would you do if you could double or triple your income this year? Would you buy a boat? Travel more? Upgrade to the newest model of luxury sedan or sports car? Taking advantage of the marketing tools that today's technology offers can help you to find prospects and customers, and then turn around and sell them your service and/or products. Thanks to the Internet, you can create raving fans with open wallets who are eager and ready to pay you money - IF you can capture their attention.

My background in Internet marketing has made me an authority on what it takes to create a cohesive marketing plan that will attract Internet customers. Here is an overview of the basic steps for targeting your market, specifically and affordably. I created the **Zbiz Marketing Manifesto** to help you succeed in today's technological age. Following my program will help you to grow your business and your income. What you do with all the profits you'll earn is up to you!

The first step is to determine exactly who your customer is and what you can offer them.

• Know Your Customer

*The Internet is **crushing** traditional forms of advertising such as newspapers and TV. Knowing your customer is very important because knowing **who you are marketing to** and what their wants, needs, and desires are is critical to selling them services or items.*

• Demographic Surveys

From Macintosh to McDonalds, all of the Fortune 500 companies use demographic surveys to get to know their customers better, and to understand what targeting practices they need to continue or change.

• Likes or Dislikes

*The psychology of human beings tells us that we will always move towards what we like and move away from what we dislike. Discovering your target audience's **likes and dislikes** will enable you to gear your marketing towards what will appeal to them.*

• Job History

Being aware of a customer or prospect's job history will help you to understand what that person's goals are. If your customer has been stuck at a dead end corporate job, you could gear your marketing message toward showing them how they can work from home and make more than they were making at their desk job.

- **Relationships and Associations**

    If you know a prospect or customer's relationship status, you can market to his needs more effectively. For example, if your prospect is married with two kids, an offer might read "Make extra money for your kids' college education."

- **Understanding Customers of other Companies**

    If you know that particular customers of a different company purchased a 5-day workshop on TV sales, you can market other products and services in TV sales to them.

The next important step of The ZBIZ Marketing Manifesto is to add more value to the service or product you are selling. This means **"being cool"** to the customer by giving them more bang for their buck.

- **Throw in Bonuses**

    *This will increase the **perceived value** of your products or services overall - giving* your customer more than they would get from "the guys across the street." Good bonuses can be informational products or training. This will give them a taste of what you can do for them and show that you care about them.

- **Make your customers feel like they are getting lucky!**

  An example of a famous person who used these techniques is the late pitchman, Billy Mays. He was exceptional at adding bonuses to the products he was selling. Billy made his customers feel like they were getting lucky by getting more for less.

- **Build a List**

  Build a list of prospects and customers who are interested in what you are selling or saying. Staying in contact with these people on **a regular basis** is important because it lets the consumer know that you are there and you care about them, especially when they are ready to buy from you.

- **Educate your prospects through content marketing**

  This would include using **keywords** in your marketing strategies to help get your service or product out there. You can use Google's keyword tool to help you determine the best *keywords for the service or product you are marketing.*

• Producing Viral Content

If you are not on top of what is "COOL" at this moment, you will have a hard time connecting with your prospects and customers. Staying on top of trendy topics and content is essential to successful Internet marketing, due to the Internet's free flow of information at record speed.

Wonderful resources for viral content are Google.com/trends, Twitter.com/trends, and mainstream media sources like CNN and Fox News.

• Be everywhere your customers are!

Knowing your customers well also means being WHERE your customers are! Being up-to-date on trendy topics will help you to determine where your customers are and what they are enjoying.

Use search engines to find out what your customers and prospects are up to. Researching trends and happenings in your industry is helpful when you need to communicate with and address the needs of your clients and prospects.

- **Matching your messaging to your market**

  Match your messaging to your market. The more appropriate you are in your messaging, the more your prospects will enjoy your advertising and marketing efforts.

- **Provide a guarantee with your service or product**

  If you look at Maslow's Hierarchy of Needs, you will discover that one of the foundations of this psychological principle is "safety." Eliminating any consumer risk to using your service or product will help someone feel more secure about making a purchase.

Overall, you can see that knowing your customer is the cornerstone of Internet marketing. Attaching more value to what you sell increases your ability to sell your products and services. Building a list and educating your prospects through greater, consistent, targeted messages increases communication and helps to establish trust.

The ability to be everywhere your customers are helps to establish your presence and also helps in understanding your customers - their likes and dislikes. Matching your messaging to your market shows that you know what you're talking about and that you care. Providing a guarantee helps with the human need for security and shows your customers and prospects you are 100% behind your product or service.

As you can see, the ZBIZ Marketing Manifesto spells out the keys to internet marketing success. By following this program, you will achieve your goals and enjoy increased income by developing your business at the speed of information. What you choose to do with that is up to you; you are only limited by your imagination!

Robin Jay is in demand as a Business Relationship Expert who shares the nuts-and-bolts of building *profitable business relationships.*

Her clients affectionately nicknamed her the *"The Queen of the Business Lunch,"* which led her to write her award-winning signature book, **The Art of the Business Lunch**, now in twelve languages. Her newest work, **B Face 2 Face 4 Success**, brings essential elements – including social media and technology – into the business relationship mix to help professionals build their most committed, productive, and profitable relationships ever.

Robin has been featured internationally on **MSNBC-TV, Newsweek, the BBC, CNN, Forbes.com, The New York Times**, and more. For more information on Robin, please visit:

> *Website:* *www.RobinJay.com*
> *E-mail:* *Robin@RobinJay.com*
> *Twitter:* *@lunchwriter*
> *LinkedIn:* *RobinJay*
> *Facebook:* *RobinJay*
> *Phone:* *702-460-1420*

Chapter Twenty-Four

Open Your House, Open Your Heart

Robin Jay

I recently was talking about business with my friend, Phil Robertson, a marketing consultant. We were discussing the importance of relationships in business, and how the most successful people understand the need to socialize with their clients and prospects. We both believe that, in the end, *whoever has the most names on their contact list wins!*

As **"The Queen of the Business Lunch,"** I highly advocate breaking bread with clients as a means of building relationships. It breaks down barriers and helps us to create solid, productive, long-lasting friendships.

Phil paused for a moment as the realization hit him. He shared, *"You know ... now that I think about it, I've **NEVER lost a client** who has been to my home for dinner!"* He proved my point that once you cross that line with a client and become friends – or at least friendly – with them, your relationship will forever be transformed. You will begin to see each other as individuals as you expose a bit of your vulnerability and humanness.

Connecting with each other

In his book **"Who's Got Your Back?"** Keith Ferrazzi wrote, "If we want to be as successful as we know we can be, we need the help of others." He shared, "As a society, we're crying out for more community, more help, more advice and support."

I've always maintained that the best way to succeed is to build relationships. I argue that the very technology that was designed to help us seems to have consumed us, instead. Everyone is pulled in so many directions – texting, instant messaging, e-mailing, and talking on their cell phones – that there is a serious **disconnect on a deeper social level.** When was the last time you had lunch or dinner with a colleague or associate and looked each other in the eye and shared ideas – WITHOUT at least one of you checking your Blackberry or iPhone for messages?

Home is where the heart is

The advantage to having a client to your home for dinner is that you will get to know each other on a more personal level - a higher level than you could attain by merely meeting at a restaurant or in an office setting.

Remember, there is a big difference between entertaining clients and hosting friends. One is work. It is more fun than a day at the office, but it is still work. When I have friends over, I can relax and be myself. When I have clients over, it's up to me to make sure everyone has a great time; I feel an increased sense of responsibility.

Hosting a dinner party can be like casting a movie; you need to invite people whom you believe will have a lot to share. Knowing how to generate stimulating conversations is nearly a lost art. Stack the deck in your favor by inviting some special friends along with your clients – friends who are entertaining, funny, or smart. It's important to have these "aces" up your sleeve! They will round out your mix of guests and keep the conversation flowing.

If you're married, make sure your spouse understands the importance of an evening with clients. If you are single, be sure to invite a savvy friend to be your "right arm." When entertaining clients, you need to be a bit more "on guard." This means attending to your guests' needs with greater attention, making sure no one gets drunk, and assuring that the evening is flowing smoothly and everyone is made to feel at ease.

The actual party: who, what, when, and why

I know that not everyone shares my passion for hours in the kitchen, preceded by hours of shopping at various grocery and specialty stores. But entertaining clients in your home doesn't have to be a formal gourmet feast that will leave you physically and financially depleted! There are many ways to make entertainment easy when opening up your home to clients and colleagues.

If you are too busy to entertain or you simply don't know how to cook, you can always hire a caterer. ***You don't need a thing – except a credit card!*** Did you know that most caterers can bring their own dishes, silverware, glassware, and even tables and chairs to your home? All you need is a small kitchen and an area large enough for your guests to sit comfortably.

When I turned forty, I was living in a very small house. I wanted to enjoy my birthday and not worry about cooking. I had about fifty guests coming over to my tiny home and wanted everyone to have a blast. I hired a Cordon Bleu-trained chef to cater the cocktail party at my home.

She showed up with two assistants and they went right to work. A friend volunteered to be the bartender; she set up the bar outside. Another friend, a massage therapist, offered chair massages. Another friend showed up with a lion cub, so everyone got a great photo keepsake. The bottom line was that this bash cost me just about $700, including alcohol. It was such a memorable event that many of my friends and clients still talk about it to this day.

Opening your home to guests doesn't even have to cost that much. When I was starting out in business, I would host pot luck suppers. To add to the fun, I would assign a theme. For example, once I had everyone bring a dish that was representative of his or her international heritage. If you decide to host a pot luck supper, be sure to specify which course each guest should bring or you could end up with twenty desserts!

You can host an Academy Award party, a murder mystery, a football party, or even the launch of any new movie on DVD. Your menu can range from pizza and chicken wings to filet mignon and cocktail attire. I threw some extremely memorable parties back when I barely earned enough to cover my mortgage. You just have to get a little bit more creative!

Fun and games....and prizes!

I had attended a party many years ago where the host had us play an icebreaker game. You are probably familiar with those at mixers, but did you ever think of doing one in your home?

Our host had full page ads taped up around the house. The ads were numbered 1 – 20 and had the names of the products they featured blackened or cut out. We were to make a list, also numbered 1 – 20, and fill in the names of the products that were advertised. I don't know about you, but I can't tell a bottle of Glenfiddich from Glenlivet! I did, however, get Dr. Scholl's, Secret, Buick, and many others. What a fun game! It gets everyone mingling and talking.

I've played that game at many parties at my house and it's always a hit. The winner gets a bottle of wine or a gift card. It's interesting to see the Type A personalities negotiating: "I'll trade you #7 if you'll tell me what #12 is!" One time, I had an ad for Tiffany & Co., their signature blue box and white bow, but without the "Tiffany & Co." logo visible. Can you believe that people were calling the "1-800" phone number in the ad to see who answered? My, but some of us sure are competitive! I still hear about that game. It takes a lot of preparation, but it's worth it.

The best part about having clients visit you at your home is that they will come to see you as an individual – not just a salesperson, coach, consultant, or vendor. They will see your design tastes, meet your spouse or friends, and – most importantly – they will feel special because you thought to invite them.

Sharing the love

I love to cook and bake. It's the perfect antidote to a long day at the computer. I am a foodie – I even enjoy watching cooking shows while I'm exercising. Once, my personal trainer noticed I had a cooking show on TV while I was on the elliptical cross-trainer. He watched for a moment as the host stirred cream into a pan of butter. He shook his head as he walked away and mumbled, "That's just WRONG!" I defended it, though, and promised to substitute fat-free "Half & Half" for the heavy cream.

I also love to try new recipes, but living alone means I could be eating a dish for several nights. It makes perfect sense to have guests over to enjoy my experiments! After all, if it's a disaster, relief in the form of pizza delivery is just a phone call away. We need to stretch ourselves and enjoy the process.

Give it a shot and schedule a dinner party. What have you got to lose? If doing this really takes you outside of your comfort zone, practice on your friends first. Here are some tips to help you execute an evening party at home successfully:

Whether you choose to do the cooking or hire a caterer, relentless preparation will pay off in spades.

- Plan your menu - from drinks to dessert.

- OVERESTIMATE the food you will need. You can always freeze leftovers, but at least no one will leave hungry.

- Clean your house, as well as your front and back yard or patio.

- Have a great back-up dish if you're trying a new recipe.

- Plan some fun or entertainment – games, karaoke, magic, etc.

The more you can do ahead of time, the more YOU will be able to enjoy the evening with your guests. There's no better way to make people feel special than by welcoming them into your home to share a meal.

NOTES

The Power of the Platform:
Speakers on Life

To order additional copies of

The Power of the Platform

please visit us at

www.ThePoweroethePlatform.com

702-460-1420

Volume discounts available

Are you a speaker?
For information on becoming a
published author, e-mail:
Robin@LVCSB.com

Engage your passion - Live the life of your dreams
Do what you love, help others, and make money!

The Las Vegas Convention Speakers Bureau
offers coaching on speaking, writing, publishing,
and marketing. Our team of experts can help you to
achieve all of your speaking and publishing goals.

The Las Vegas Convention Speakers Bureau
www.LVCSB.com

Are you a meeting planner?
How did YOUR last meeting leave them feeling?
Hire a PROFESSIONAL and Feel the Electricity!

The Las Vegas Convention Speakers Bureau
provides professional keynote speakers for
conventions, conferences, seminars, and meetings.

*We've got the speakers you need on
today's hottest topics, including:*
*social media, sales, attitude, networking,
leadership, communication, customer service,
humor, marketing, relationships, adversity, ethics,
diversity, and more.*
*Call or e-mail the
Las Vegas Convention Speakers Bureau
Today!*

*For a FREE E-book
Visit: www.LVCSB.com/FreeEbook/*
The Las Vegas Convention Speakers Bureau
www.LVCSB.com

LAS VEGAS
CONVENTION
SPEAKERS BUREAU
~ Featuring World-Class Speakers
Robin@LVCSB.com
www.LVCSB.com
702-460-1420